BAITS and
ARTIFICIAL LURES

First published 1993 by Boxtree Limited

This edition published 2001 by Boxtree
an imprint of Macmillan Publishers Ltd
25 Eccleston Place London SW1W 9NF
Basingstoke and Oxford
Associated companies throughout the world
www.macmillan.com

ISBN 0 7522 1929 4

1 3 5 7 9 8 6 4 2

A CIP catalogue record for this book is available from
the British Library.

Designed by Anita Ruddell
Printed and bound in the E.C.

BAITS and ARTIFICIAL LURES

JOHN WILSON

BOXTREE

From his own well stocked, lily-clad lakes in deepest Norfolk, John practises what he preaches, catching carp on a variety of natural and manufactured baits.

CONTENTS

ACKNOWLEDGEMENTS

I would like to thank the editing and design team, the mates who leave their own fishing to photograph me, and a very special thank you to Dave Batten who has made such a fine job of the line illustrations.

John Wilson 1993

FOREWORD

In our prepacked world, where the convenience factor continues to affect even the baits we use for fishing, there is more reason than ever for 'going back to nature' and, where possible, exploring some of the old values. For instance, simply gathering your own baits is one of the true delights of fishing, providing through a valuable learning curve a greater knowledge of natural history and even increased catches of difficult species.

They say there is nothing new in fishing, and taking the bait scene as a whole, there is much truth in this adage. For instance, even boilies, which, together with shop-bought maggots, are by far the most commonly used of all freshwater baits today, evolved as a replacement for parboiled potatoes, the skin of which protects them from nuisance species pecking away until a carp happens along. But potatoes will still catch, and are especially worth a try in waters where the carp have never seen them, because they will have no reason to treat them with suspicion, as they do all the more common offerings.

This is what bait selection is really all about: choosing one which is readily available, yet of which the fish are not already suspicious. So be adventurous and always willing to experiment.

John Wilson
Great Witchingham
1993

CHAPTER ONE

NATURAL BAITS

Because many natural baits are either part of a river's ecosystem, or live close by and therefore often find their way into the water, as worms do during floods, for instance, fish come to accept them as part of their natural diet and show far less caution than they do to manufactured baits.

Varying little in format from their freshwater counterparts, even natural baits from the sea, such as cockles, prawns and shrimps, are devoured with equal relish, while the shop-bought maggot closely resembles the grub-like larvae of countless species of aquatic insects which live out their yearly cycle on the bottom of lakes and rivers everywhere as the staple diet of most fish of the carp family, or cyprinids. Many natural baits, both terrestrial and water-borne, also have the benefit of being entirely free. Gathering them vastly increases the angler's awareness of natural history, and he can only be a better all-round fisherman with such knowledge.

There is also a greater sense of achievement from catching fish on naturals which have been collected solely for use as fishing bait. Permanently kept in the boot of my car is a strong, rectangular-framed, micromesh net (available from any aquarium

Lobworms can be obtained in a number of ways: by searching the lawn or local cricket pitch at night with a torch, following a good downpour; by digging the garden over; or simply by observing seagulls following the plough.

By collecting lob-worms during periods of wet weather and storing them in his wormery, John can go perch fishing anytime — even during high summer when the ground has been dry for weeks.

Carp working their way through sub-merged marginal sedges and reeds or lilies are absolute suckers for a freelined lobworm. And if you cannot achieve the distance with one worm, then put two up on a size 4 hook tied direct to the reel line.

9

shop) with a 24-in handle; a one-gallon plastic bucket with a pull–off lid with plenty of air holes, which will hold anything from caddis grubs to slugs; and a torch. All three items, which together cost less than three pints of maggots, have frequently provided me with natural baits when far from civilization and even purchasing a loaf of bread was out of the question. The point is, if you always restrict yourself to shop-bought maggots, casters or boilies, you could find yourself at a loss should the chance of an impromptu session suddenly present itself.

For certain species, chub in particular, heavy natural baits such as a big, fat slug or a lobworm simply have no equal for both casting and catching during the summer and autumn. I personally would feel at a great disadvantage if I did not collect these and many other natural baits for use on a regular basis when river fishing.

Terrestrial baits

Lobworms

I can't think of a freshwater species that I haven't caught on lobworms, not only in Britain but in freshwater the world over. It is probably the closest thing there is to a universal bait. Barbel, tench, perch, eels, catfish, chub and big bream all bolt lobs down greedily, and under certain circumstances there is no finer bait for specimen roach. Wait until the river has been over the banks for a few days and is running like strong tea, then leger or stret-peg a lobworm on a size 8 hook close into the bank, and you could prove the point.

Lobworms are also a superb bait for carp, which react rapidly to the gyrating movements of a lob freelined among lily pads, into a scum line or beneath overhanging willow branches. Wherever dense bottom weeds prove troublesome with other baits, try injecting a little air from a hypodermic syringe into the head of the lob and adjust the hooklength to the weed's height so that the bait floats easily visible, above the weed. Tench and big bream fall for this technique too.

You must, of course, first collect your lobs. Freshly dug vegetable and flower beds are an excellent source of worms. So is, for those of you who live in the country, a newly ploughed field. Hundreds of seagulls seem to appear from nowhere when in mild, damp weather worms by the thousand are turned over in this way. A few polite words to the farmer could result in a tinful within minutes. But don't simply go marching across the field; always ask first.

My favourite method of collecting worms by the hundred is to visit the local cricket pitch after dark (as night falls worms start to come up out of their holes) following a good downpour. If rain has been falling steadily for a few days, all the better. Wait until it has stopped or reduced to a fine drizzle —

10

these are the best worm-collecting conditions of all — and worms will be lying there, most of them out of their holes, just waiting to be picked up with the aid of a wide-beam torch of medium power. Don't use a powerful spot-beam torch, or they will disappear in a flash. Try not to engage in a tug of war with every worm whose tail is firmly down its hole when you grip hold of the head. Pulled or stretched lobworms are fine for the next day's fishing only, but should not be kept for future use in case they die and contaminate the others.

For ease of collecting lobs, hang a one-gallon plastic bucket on a strap around your neck at chest height. Also, don't scrape your feet when walking, as the vibrations will have the worms scurrying down their holes long before the torch beam catches them. Creep along, raising each foot like a strutting cockerel. It may look stupid, but if you want a bucketful of worms, it is worth the effort of being stealthy.

For fishing sessions I like to pack lobworms into fresh sphagnum moss with plenty of room to spare inside a two-pint bait box. Another excellent medium for transporting them in is sopping-wet, shredded newspaper. This was a tip passed on to me by my old mate, Fred J. Taylor after one of his many trips to the USA, where they call worms 'night crawlers' and keep them in hotel-like comfort. To 'condition' lobs, as the Americans say, put freshly gathered worms (a dozen to a bait box on the assumption that if one dies you can lose no more than another 11) into a two-pint bait box containing strips of wet newspaper. Tear the paper into 1-in strips and soak it thoroughly in a bowl of cold water before squeezing out some (not all) of the water. When all the bait boxes have their dozen or so worms in wet newsprint, simply leave them in the fridge (if you have an understanding partner) until required. They may be left for several weeks, but after a week their 'conditioning' is usually complete and inside will be the fattest, most superb lobworms you have ever seen.

An important part of keeping lobworms is not allowing them to become hot. Below 0°C (32°F) they freeze, while above 10°C (50°F) they will deteriorate quite quickly. A temperature somewhere in between — hence the fridge — is ideal. Something you might like to try is making a lobworm storage box for holding up to several hundred worms at a time (see diagram). This is constructed from $\frac{1}{2}$-in marine ply cut into four squares of 20 x 20 in (the sides) and two pieces of 21 x 20 in (the lids). Air holes of $\frac{1}{8}$ in in diameter are drilled through the sides of the box and an inside rim of 1 x $\frac{1}{2}$-in softwood is nailed and glued to the inside of both lids to form a seal.

Inside the box put masses of newspaper strips (you need lots of old papers) well-soaked and wrung out, followed immediately by the fresh lobworms. I can't overstress the word 'fresh' here, for dead worms all too rapidly contaminate the others.

11

Pack a dozen or so to each two pint bait box filled with sopping wet torn newspaper strips and leave them to chill for a week in the fridge for lobworms conditioned to absolute perfection.

Below: Lobworm storage box.

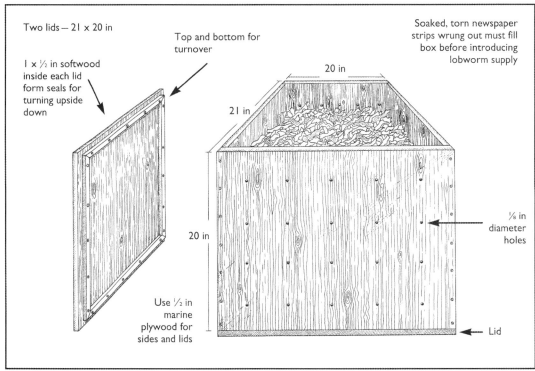

Two lids — 21 x 20 in

Top and bottom for turnover

Soaked, torn newspaper strips wrung out must fill box before introducing lobworm supply

1 x ½ in softwood inside each lid form seals for turning upside down

20 in

21 in

⅛ in diameter holes

20 in

Use ½ in marine plywood for sides and lids

Lid

Keep the box on a concrete or stone floor, in the garage for instance, and in subdued light. Every three or four days simply turn the entire box over carefully and the worms, now at the top, will work their way through the wet newspaper down to the bottom again. Provided it is kept cool, this 'lobwormery' will keep worms fresh and ready for use for many weeks.

Wet shredded newspaper is an excellent medium for transporting any kind of worm when travelling abroad, should Customs prohibit taking peat, soil or moss into the country. Anyone travelling to the Republic of Ireland, for instance, could have their entire stock of worms confiscated if they are packed in an organic medium.

Dendrobenas

The next worm down in size from the lobworm is the Dendrobena, a chunky 3-in red worm imported to Britain from the Netherlands, where it is very common. These worms are just the right size for perch, tench and bream, and are available from most good tackle shops ready packed in plastic boxes with around 15 worms in each. This may not seem many, but since they are at least twice as thick as brandlings, just one worm on the hook offers the fish a good mouthful. I am sure I have occasionally come across exactly the same species of

It may seem strange but king ragworms and lugworms from saltwater make a great change bait for freshwater species like eels, perch, chub and pike.

13

worm when moving old, rotten logs and the like, but never in great enough quantity to guarantee a supply of them for bait.

Brandlings

This lively, gyrating worm, easily recognizable by the yellowy-orange rings around its tail and the pungent yellow fluid which seeps out as you hook it, can be obtained in three ways. The cheapest is to politely ask a farmer if you can collect a supply by turning over his manure heaps. If this turns out to be a regular occurrence, saving you many pounds over a season, don't forget to drop him off a bottle of Christmas cheer.

Brandlings are also readily available from most tackle shops and usually come packed in peat at around 50 to a tub. But you might prefer to make your own wormery cum compost heap at the bottom of the garden from both garden and household waste, so as to have a supply of worms readily available throughout the season. If so, start it off with two tubs of brandlings from the tackle shop.

Present one or two brandlings on a size 12 hook or a bunch on a size 10. To stop them wriggling over the barb and off the hook, tip it with a single maggot, caster or kernel of sweetcorn. Alternatively, after the worms, slip on a small section cut from a wide rubber band. Perch, tench, bream, rudd, grayling and especially crucian carp all love brandlings.

Redworms

These short, slow-moving worms are lovers of compost heaps consisting mainly of rotting leaves rather than manure. Wherever piles of leaves have been stacked and left to break down, forming a rich leaf-mould, redworms provide a regular source of bait. All cyprinids love them, especially tench, bream, dace and chub. And for long-trotting for grayling there is no finer bait. Present one on a size 14 hook, two on a 12 and so on, or offer them as a cocktail in conjunction with corn, casters, maggots or a crust cube, for instance. Because these worms do not wriggle off the hook, they are ideal for use in combination with spinners. (See Spinners, page 126).

Lugworms and Ragworms

If you live near the coast and can obtain a fresh supply of either lugworms or ragworms, or your inland tackle dealer stocks them, don't assume that only sea fish love them. Expensive they may be, but as an entirely different change bait for species such as carp, tench, chub and bream, both worms produce results.

Use lugworms as you would a big lobworm, freelined on a size 6 or 4 hook — chub devour them greedily. Ragworms, especially the thick-bodied 'king rag' (watch out for its pincers) are best cut into 1–1½ in segments with even smaller bits thrown in as loose feed. I haven't tried them, but as other sea baits such as squid produce well, these worms could prove effective for catfish. Both worms are best kept in the fridge (if possible, wrapped individually in clean newspaper) and you should change the paper daily. Of the two, ragworms will last much longer — up to a week or so.

Mealworms

This popular live food source, bred specifically for rearing birds, reptiles and mammals, has been available to the pet trade for many years, and is now being marketed for the fisherman. Mealworms make a super bait. The largest supplier is the Mealworm Company, which channels its products through specialist tackle shops, offering British-bred mealworms in four sizes, from 'minis' to the 'super giant'. The latter, presented two up on a size 8 hook, is heavy enough for freelining to chub.

Buff-coloured, looking like a cross between a caterpillar and a maggot — in fact not unlike a caddis grub — mealworms are actually the larvae of a beetle, and are extremely active. The larger ones have a similar thrashing action to brandlings, making them attractive to all cyprinids.

Mealworms last much longer than unrefrigerated maggots: at least for several weeks if kept in the bran-filled plastic containers in which they are sold. Alternatively, transfer them to a large, open, smooth-sided bucket or tray with around ½ in of fresh bran in the bottom. Don't bother with a lid for tall containers. A temperature of around 10°C (50°F) seems to suit them perfectly, although the 'super giant' mealworm requires a higher temperature of between 16 and 21°C (60–70°F).

Being little larger than a fat bloodworm, the 'mini' mealworm is ideal for very light float fishing and size 18–20 hooks, in conjunction with loose-fed pinkies or squatts. The standard mealworm as hookbait couples nicely with loose-fed maggots or casters and size 16 or 14 hooks. The two largest mealworms have all sorts of possibilities when presented on hooks in sizes from 12 to 6: for perch, carp, barbel and tench. They are a marvellous natural bait, and well worth a try.

Wasp Grubs and Nests

While wasp grubs readily catch dace, roach, grayling and even the occasional barbel, chub are driven absolutely wild, sometimes into an unbelievable feeding frenzy (through careful loose-feeding) by the sweet and sickly aroma of both grubs and the grub-laden cakes which make up the football-sized nest. These cakes, around ¾ in thick and exactly the size of a round two-pint bait box, may even be frozen until needed. When defrosted (as opposed to fresh), the grubs will be next to useless as hookbaits, but you can feed in mashed-up cake and use this in conjunction with a waxworm or a tebo on the hook (see Waxworms and Tebos, page 18). Alternatively, for enticing

15

Available at most pet shops, and even specialist tackle centres, mealworms come in various sizes to suit any situation, be it trotting for roach and dace or freelining for chub.

Opposite: Looking to all intents and purposes like giant, succulent maggots, it is small wonder that tench turn on quickly to mealworms, whether legered or presented on a lift-method float rig.

chub to the surface during the summer, carefully break the cake, frozen or fresh, into $1\frac{1}{2}$ - in squares and freeline it on a size 6 hook.

Wasp cake is far better used fresh, so to enjoy this superb bait, which has truly magical qualities for chub, you must find a source of freshly killed nests. Throughout July and August the cakes are more liable to be packed full of grubs and so they are best harvested at this time. Most good hardware shops stock special preparations, such as Rentokil products, for effectively killing the nest. The directions for use must be followed to the letter.

When fishing, keep your eyes open for wasps which disappear into the bank. Or you may see them in your garden, since rockeries and any other quiet piece of bank are prime locations. But if you don't fancy killing your own nests, make a polite request to fruit farmers in July, when, in the process of reducing the wasp population while the cakes are heavily laden with fat grubs, numerous nests are destroyed. Local councils may also hold the key to obtaining a supply of nests. Simply ring the Pest Control Department.

Waxworms

Waxworms are the larvae of the waxmoth, which infests beehives to lay its eggs in the honeycombs. A fat, juicy, fairly buoyant, creamy-white grub similar in size to a wasp grub, the waxworm fits nicely on a size 14 or 12 hook (hook it carefully

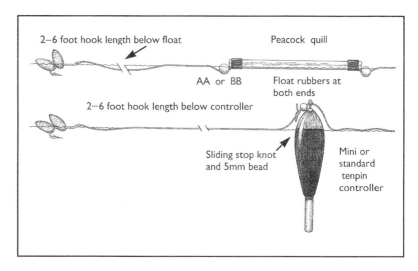

2–6 foot hook length below float

Peacock quill

AA or BB

Float rubbers at both ends

2–6 foot hook length below controller

Sliding stop knot and 5mm bead

Mini or standard tenpin controller

through the tail end). This makes it especially effective when trotting for grayling, dace, roach and chub in conjunction with loose-fed maggots or with mashed-up wasp cake when good grubs are in short supply. Waxworms keep well in the tub provided, at a temperature of between 13 and 16°C (55–60°F). It is worth checking regularly and removing any dead ones so that the rest do not spoil. Bred specifically for the live pet-food trade, waxworms are also available through specialist tackle shops.

Tebos

If you catch fish on 'super giant' mealworms, then you will love these even larger grubs. They are the larvae of a moth imported from Chile, which feeds on the fibrous soft wood beneath the bark of the tebo tree. Tebos come packed in bran and will last up to three weeks if stored at between 7 and 10°C (45 –50°F). Being larger than a wasp grub, they are a superb hookbait for long-trotting when loose-feeding with maggots or mashed-up wasp cake, and are best presented singly on a size 12 hook or two up on a 10. Chub adore them.

Grubs and Caterpillars

Any large, weighty caterpillar of either moths or butterflies — and there are dozens — makes a superb freelining bait for chub. Hook it very carefully through the head on a size 10 or 8 hook and cast gently. If distance is required, use in conjunction with a mini floating controller such as the tenpin (see diagram).

Beetle Larvae

One of the largest, fattest, most succulent and more importantly, when weight is required for freelining for carp or chub, one of the heaviest of larvae, is that of both the stag beetle and the lesser stag beetle. Up to 2 in long and ½ in thick, these white larvae have a distinctive, orange-chestnut head and front legs and lie in a curled-up position for up to three years during the second stage of metamorphosis, the first stage being the eggs laid by the adult beetle. In the third stage the larva changes into a pupa during the autumn, but does not complete the cycle until the following spring, when the adult beetle emerges by chewing its way out of the rotten wood.

Stag beetles lay their eggs in rotting fallen trees and in old fungi-covered tree stumps, particularly of ash, elm, oak and silver birch. Prise the rotten outer layers of wood away carefully to reveal the huge grubs curled up in their separate chambers. When you find one, there could be up to a couple of dozen baits in the same log. So that the internal juices do not burst, hook the grub once only through the head with a size 8 hook tied direct, and cast gently.

Another useful large white grub is that of the nocturnal cockchafer, found by pulling up turfs or simply digging over the garden. It feeds on plant roots for two or three years during the larva stage, and, like stag-beetle grubs, sports a chestnut-coloured head and lies in a curled-up position. Present it on a size 8 hook, gently nicked through the head.

Leatherjackets

Feeding just beneath the surface of the ground on the roots of many plants and grasses, leatherjackets are the grey, maggot-like larvae of the long-legged crane-fly (better known as the daddy-long-legs) and hatch by the thousand during the autumn. Leatherjackets can be used for roach, dace and chub on float tackle, presented singly on a size 14 hook or two up on a size 12. Alternatively, catch the live daddy-long-legs and carefully mount it on a size 14 or 12 hook, presenting it with a surface controller float to obtain distance. Grease the line between the hook and controller (see diagram).

Grasshoppers, House Crickets and Locusts

For chub enthusiasts, whether dapping at close range from an entanglement of marginal cover or floating them downstream on the surface with a greased line and controller float such as the tenpin (see diagram), grasshoppers, house crickets and locusts are wonderful natural baits for use during the warmer months, especially in high summer, when weed growth makes legering almost impossible.

If you don't want to run about chasing grasshoppers, or there are never any in the field beside the river when you want them, invest in some medium-sized locusts or large house crickets, both of which are available from pet shops which specialize in live foods. They are bred to feed spiders, lizards, frogs and certain large birds, and may easily be kept in an old aquarium until required. Make sure that the lid is well ventilated

19

Once you have located the wasps' nest, a liberal coating of the special 'killing' dust should be squirted deep inside each entrance hole after dark, when all the wasps have retired.

When digging out a 'killed' nest, try to remove it in its whole state, which is about the size of a football, comprising several 'cakes' ¾ in thick. Unfortunately, this nest was situated below a thick tree root and had to be removed in chunks.

20

The hornets' nest is chub bait supreme — much rarer and even better than wasps' nests because the succulent grubs are considerably larger. Use grub-laden chunks on the surface, freelined through the swim, or present a single grub on trotting tackle while loose feeding with the same.

Heavy enough for freelining to chub or carp, and presented one or two up on a size 8 or 6 hook, these fat, juicy stag beetle larvae are found amongst the crumbling wood of fallen and rotten trees.

(gauze is perfect) and fits tightly and, with locusts especially, that the temperature remains at around 27°C (80°F). Large house crickets will tolerate lower temperatures, so for both the kitchen is the ideal place.

Feed locusts with fresh grass daily and house crickets with fresh potato or other vegetable peelings, from which they extract liquid. Your local live-food stockist will give you further advice.

The best way to present these baits so that they remain alive and active, thus luring chub out from even the darkest hide-out, is to gently ease the hook through the rear end, directly opposite the back legs. Locusts sit nicely on a size 8 hook, and house crickets on a size 10, as does the average-sized grasshopper.

Slugs

While I have purposely caught specimen dace on small white slugs, and had the occasional perch or pike lunge into a large slug being twitched back upstream through the swim, slugs are really the prime bait for one species and one species only: that ever-friendly glutton, the chub. During the summer and autumn I put slugs at the very top of the chub's natural bait list, since they are heavy enough to freeline quite a long way (at least 20 yards) without additional shotting. In addition, the slug often slips conveniently up the line during the fight, so that it can be used for a second or even third chub.

I particularly like slugs for summer chubbing when over-hanging foliage is dense, because they can be skate-cast — like flat pebbles at the seaside — into the most awkward spots, where the largest chub always love to lie, and invariably respond instantly. But you need to be on your toes, and heaving against that chub with a forgiving 'Avon' — action rod and 6-lb line before it even considers wrapping the hook around a snag. Slugging provides wonderful sport, and is the most exciting of all the mobile freelining techniques available to the summer chubber.

Slugs will also take chub if legered into deep runs or pools where the water is too turbulent or too deep for freelining. But either way, always use a large hook such as a size 4, preferably a long-shank, tied direct to the reel line. Nick the slug once only through one end, just through the leathery outer skin so that the juices do not seep out and shrink it to half its original size.

Most British slugs are vegetarians, as gardeners know only too well, but there is a carnivorous species which sports a tiny shell on its rear end (proving its ancestry with snails) that lives underground, where it feeds on earthworms.

For the chub fisherman, however, there are three species of large slugs (2–4 in long) which are particularly suited to freelining. The common red slug is easily identified by an orange frill to the underside of its brown body. The great grey slug, a most distinctive creature, is flecked with dark-brown markings over a pale grey body. But everyone's favourite is the black slug, although I doubt whether the colour makes any real difference. Provided the slug is heavy enough to cast easily and makes a resounding 'dinner is served' plop on the surface, chub come a-running.

If slugs have a drawback, it is trying to find them just when you want them. They are certainly creatures of the night, although during heavy rain among thick vegetation they can be found away from their crevice hide-outs in reasonable numbers. The secret (as with lobworms) is to gather a whole batch of slugs when conditions are suitable and they are plentiful, and keep them in an old aquarium until required.

Search in compost heaps, beneath damp sacking (leave a pile of old sacks in a quiet, dark corner of the garden for this purpose) beneath large rockery stones, in damp cellars or under piles of old logs. In fact, any damp, rotting hidey-hole can prove fruitful. Ensure that the aquarium is fitted with a tight, well-ventilated lid, and introduce a batch of slugs, along with an amount of fresh vegetation for them to eat. Keep it in a cool, dark spot such as the garage, cellar, garden shed or outhouse, and you will always have a superb supply of chubbing baits to hand.

Snails

Just about everything I have said about slugs as bait applies equally to the larger land snails, of which there are over 80 British species. As with slugs, you can even keep snails you have gathered in an old aquarium. The only difference is that immediately before use you crack the shell and peel it off, allowing the hook to be nicked once only through the outer skin.

True, snails lack the casting weight of slugs once the shell has gone, but this can be remedied by presenting two, or even three, on a size 8 or 6 hook tied direct to 5 or 6–lb line.

I doubt whether chub can really tell the difference between snails and slugs, and certainly snails have on numerous occasions provided me with a chubbing bait when slugs were in short supply.

Maggots

Because they are readily available from all tackle shops at a reasonable price and are instantly attractive to all species of cyprinids, maggots are easily the most popular of all natural, land-borne baits for use in freshwater.

Standard Maggots as Hookbait

The standard maggot stocked by tackle shops are bred specifically from the second most common European bluebottle, and come already coloured either mixed or in single colours: yellow, pink, green, red, bronze and, of course, plain white. Many breeders introduce colour to the fish, chicken or turkey carcasses on which maggots are fed, but colouring white, shop-bought maggots yourself is easy with non-carcinogenic liquid dyes such as the Spectra range.

Riddle off any bran, sawdust or maize meal and dead maggots using a ⅛-in riddle and put the maggots in a shallow tray. Sprinkle a capful of dye over them and wait for half an hour for the maggots to work their way in and spread the colour evenly. Finally, add half a pint of maize meal to each pint of maggots to stop them sweating, and use them straight away or store them. Maggots are best kept in an old fridge (not the family fridge) in the garage or on the cool concrete floor of the garage itself, or in a garden shed or outhouse in open tins rather than plastic bait boxes.

If you use maggots regularly, an old fridge, which will use a minimal amount of electricity soon pays for itself. Without a fridge, however, continuing metamorphosis will rapidly turn the maggots into bluebottles. When buying maggots, look for a dark spot beneath the skin, which proves that they have been off the feed for only a few days and are really fresh. Those without a 'feed line' spot will soon be useless as a live bait, their

23

There is nothing more effective for enticing a summer chub away from its hideaway beneath overhanging trees or weed rafts than the resounding plop of a big, fat, succulent slug landing on the surface. Present slugs freelined on a size 6 or 4 hook, tied direct.

metabolic rate rapidly decreasing as they approach the formation of the chrysalis or pupa. Anglers call this form the 'caster'.

For transporting maggots abroad, or when they could end up crammed in standard bait boxes for a couple of days in warm weather before use, follow this simple procedure. Riddle off the maggots as described above and put the healthy ones in an open tray in the fridge, reducing the temperature to just a few degrees above freezing so that they are hardly moving. Then pack them into a muslin bag (up to two gallons at a time) and place in a polystyrene cold-box to which has been added six standard freezer packs of the flat type, which contain a special fluid and remain frozen for a long time. In this way, maggots will last for up to four days. On arriving at your final destination, remove the maggots and transfer them to a large, open tray, adding maize meal after an hour or so, once their meta-

bolic rate starts to increase.

To ensure maximum attraction, it is imperative that the maggots' inner juices and lifeblood do not drain out when you hook them on. Carefully nick the point of the hook through the tough, blunt end between the two tiny dots. Present one standard maggot on a size 18 or 20 hook, two on a size 16 or 14 and bunches of four to six on sizes 12 and 10. It is a bit fiddly, but when you are carp or barbel fishing with hooks that are really

Match fishing demands a comprehensive selection of maggots, from plain white, bronze and pinkie hookbaits to squatts, which are used as loose feed.

25

thick in the wire (which burst the maggots) use a 2-in stringer of, say, ½-lb monofilament or fly-tying thread tied to the eye, and with the aid of a needle, sleeve on a dozen or so maggots and tie the hair off at the bend of the hook after winding the string of maggots firmly around the shank. This arrangement looks very tempting (see diagram).

Maggots make great cocktails: maggots and brandlings or redworms, maggots and corn or stewed wheat, maggots and casters, for instance. The permutations are many. Incidentally, there may well be occasions when maggots are just too lively for their own good and wriggle quickly into the bottom sediment of silty waters such as estate lakes and meres. To counteract this when I intend swimfeedering for bream and tench, for instance, I simply scald in boiling hot water for a few seconds all the maggots to be used as loose feed, which kills and 'stretches' them instantly. Tench and bream never seem to mind, and the loose feed sits there on the bottom, along with the explosion of crumb groundbait, in full view of passing fish.

During a heatwave, when fridges often break down, everything dries and becomes stretched if you are not careful, from maggots left in your box to those stored by the gallon in huge trays by tackle dealers. But don't automatically discard dead, stretched, or even putrid, stinking maggots, because *en masse* they are a magical carp attractor.

Fortunately the cold room in my tackle shop has not overheated on many occasions over the years, but when it has, hundreds of pounds worth of maggots have been ruined. I have arrived on a Monday morning to find the cold-room motor iced up and most of the stock roasted to death and completely unsaleable after a weekend of suffocating heat. And doesn't it

Presenting maggots on a stringer.

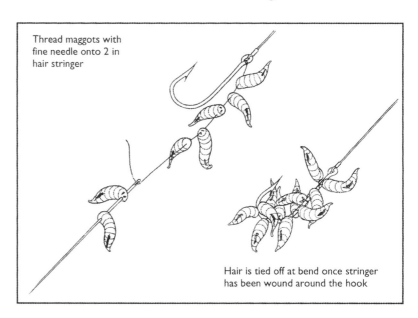

Thread maggots with fine needle onto 2 in hair stringer

Hair is tied off at bend once stringer has been wound around the hook

always occur over the weekend?

The first time this happened, rather than completely waste the stock (which, after all, dead or alive, is a protein food source) I took the entire batch home and emptied two trays each (about eight gallons) into several marginal swims in the two shallow lakes close to my house, much to the enjoyment of the syndicate members.

Within an hour, each of those swims was packed full of gorging carp, their tails literally sticking out above the surface while they stood on their heads sucking in the maggot feast. Such was their feeding frenzy, they immediately pounced on almost any bait offered. This is food for thought, because it has since been my experience that this routine works on most fisheries, even those stuffed full of small nuisance species. But you do need a vast quantity of maggots to fill everything up before the carp move in, as they eventually will.

When loose-feeding with maggots, in all but the most extreme close-range, windless conditions opt for the accuracy of a loose-feed catapult or throwing stick rather than chucking them out by hand. There is no easier way to ruin your fishing than inviting fish to chase loose feed indiscriminately hurled in well away from the swim.

Colour is a topic guaranteed to get everyone arguing over the tackle-shop counter. Some prefer plain white maggots, some simply wouldn't tackle up if bronze ones were not available, while others swear by maggots dyed red, or even fluorescent colours. Over the years I must confess to a preference for bronze maggots in cold, clear water, and dark red when fishing in peaty-coloured water — the rivers of Denmark, Sweden and Ireland, for instance. In the end I suppose it's all down to how confident you are, and if a particular colour makes you fish with greater confidence, you will undoubtedly catch.

Sucked or skinned maggots are one of the problems suffered when using this bait. Despite their having been sucked back to the cyprinids' pharyngeal (throat) teeth and crushed to pulp, you can still miss the bite. If you simply did not see a bite, try shotting the float tip down more, moving the bottom shot closer to the hook, reducing tail length between hook and leger or striking earlier, hopefully between the maggots' inner juices being sucked out and the skins spat out.

There are occasions, with the swim full of feeding bream and size 10 or 8 hooks the order of the day, when leaving four 'skins' on the hook and replacing just one or two maggots every other cast can save all the bother of rebaiting. The bream never seem to mind.

Gozzers

These maggots, noticeably softer than those you buy from the tackle shop, are the larvae of the common European bluebottle.

Wherever small species do not prove troublesome, there is no finer bait for barbel than a bunch of a dozen or so maggots gently sleeved on to a size 8 or 6 hook, as John proves with this splendid River Wensum specimen.

Maggots are the perfect bait for legering in conjunction with a block-end feeder. For a slow dispersal of the contents, ensure the feeder's holes are not too large.

Because it does not fare happily indoors, this is not bred commercially and available over the counter.

Some fishermen swear by gozzers, since bream in particular hold on to them longer because of their soft skin. So if you wish to give them a try, you need to breed enough to provide a hookbait. But it is rather a rigmarole. Wrap a chicken breast or a pig's heart loosely in newspaper and leave it in a dark, dry, cool spot in a quiet corner of the garden and wait for the fly to lay its eggs. Once the meat has a blow on it, put it into an open tin covered in gauze (protected from the rain) so that no other flies can lay on it, and leave the eggs to hatch.

Within several days the 'gozzer' maggots will have had their fill and be ready to leave the meat, which should be shaken over a $\frac{1}{8}$ in riddle into a tray containing bran or maize meal. Colour your gozzers pale bronze or golden yellow, and you have the bream maggot *par excellence*.

Pinkies

We have the shiny-backed 'greenbottle' to thank for this considerably smaller maggot, which gets its name from turning a very pale pink within hours of being taken off the feed. Many fishermen nevertheless still prefer to colour their pinkies either red or bronze, and use them as loose feed or mixed in with the groundbait while presenting a standard-sized maggot or maggots on the hook.

Being much smaller, pinkies are ideal with tiny hooks or

when you are fishing in really cold, clear water during the winter for dace, roach and bream. One pinkie fits perfectly on a size 22 or 24 hook, or two on a size 20. Remember to use only fine-wire hooks, which puncture the skin easily without bursting it, and allow the bait to behave as naturally as possible. Heavy, forged hooks weight the pinkie down, making it sink too quickly. A pinkie 'caster' and pinkie maggot together on a size 20 hook are a deadly combination over a weedy or debris-covered bottom.

Squatts

This tiny maggot, bred from the common housefly, is usually only available from tackle shops during the summer, when it is put to good use mixed in with the groundbait for bream fishing. Nowhere near so active as other maggots, it will not burrow into the bottom sediment before the bream locate it. Nowadays most bream enthusiasts prefer to lace their groundbait with casters instead of squatts, so that this tiny maggot,

Left: A bunch of casters presented on the top with the aid of the 'flat float' technique (see diagram on page 18) is a great way of encouraging bites from the quick-biting, super-wary, golden orfe. This beautiful specimen was only ounces short of 4 lb.

29

always difficult to keep, has slipped down the popularity ladder.

The squatt is the obvious match fisherman's hookbait choice wherever bloodworms are banned, and is best presented singly on a tiny size 24 fine-wire hook, or two up on a 22.

Along with pinkies, squatts are great for catching tiny fish such as gudgeon, sticklebacks, minnows and the like when you require a few small live or deadbaits for chub, perch and the like.

One small piece of advice when buying maggots over the counter, be they pinkies, squatts or standard hookbaits. *Never* cram into a bait box exactly what it will hold. Two pints of maggots crammed into a two-pint box, for instance, will not allow sufficient space and air for them to breathe, resulting in spoiled bait and wasted money unless they are used within hours. An excellent rule of thumb is to use a bait box which holds a pint of air, plus fresh maize meal to stop them from sweating, for each pint of maggots bought. Into a pint-sized box, therefore, put no more than half a pint of maggots. In the long run, extra bait boxes are far cheaper than suffocated maggots.

Casters

Once referred to as the 'chrysalis', just as before the 1960s, maggots were called 'gentles', the caster is the pupa stage of the bluebottle, during which time the maggot is eventually transformed by metamorphosis into an air-borne fly.

It is best to catch the caster during the early stages, while it is a golden yellow and the inside juices are still heavy, which ensures that it sinks. this is most easily achieved by regularly putting a batch of slow-moving maggots through an $\frac{1}{8}$ in riddle at low room temperatures during the summer. Outside, in the garage or garden shed, is ideal. In the winter, dare I suggest, unless you have a heated outhouse, doing this inside the house is best as there is an even temperature in which maggots will continue to 'turn'.

The sinking casters can be kept in two ways. The first is to put them into a bucket of water to ensure they all sink (skim off any floaters) and leave them for a few minutes, which kills the creature forming inside and so completely halts its advancement. Pack them into a polythene bag and store in the fridge for up to three or four days, during which time they should be used, otherwise, as the animal inside decays, they will start to stink. But even then all is not lost (see Groundbaits page 51).

The second method is to put the golden sinkers straight from the riddle into a bait box covered in dampened newspaper or a piece of damp towelling, and pop them straight into the coldest part of the fridge, where further metamorphosis is greatly retarded. Again, ideally they should be used within a few days before the colour darkens as the fly forms inside and they all turn into floaters.

All cyprinids love casters: dace, roach, rudd, bream, chub, barbel, tench and carp, even perch and grayling. In clear, cold water conditions, casters invariably produce a better stamp of dace, roach and chub, particularly when used with loose-fed hempseed. When they are mixed in with hempseed and deposited on the bottom with a large block-end feeder (enlarge the holes for a swift delivery) barbel soon acquire a great liking for casters. Use a bunch on a size 10 hook tipped with a brandling or redworm, or for shy barbel, two casters and a bronze maggot on a size 14 hook.

Caster cocktails in conjunction with brandlings, sweetcorn, maggots and bread are great catchers. Because of the buoyancy of dark (floating) casters, it is possible to offer both a maggot and a dark-red caster on the hook, which rises conveniently above dense bottom weeds.

Floating casters are superb surface baits. During the warmer months dace, rudd, chub and carp will all rise freely to the surface for loose-fed floaters. Present them on a flat float peacock rig or in conjunction with a mini tenpin floating controller (see diagram).

For roach, dace and chub, present standard sinking casters singly on a fine-wire size 18 or 20 hook, piercing one end with the point and gently burying the entire hook inside. With larger hooks pierce the shell carefully or it will shatter.

To stop golden casters from turning into floaters when fishing in warm weather, cover them with water in the bait box. Casters are great for mixing in with groundbait for tench and for bream because, whereas maggots wriggle and break the balls up quickly, even before you throw them out, and then disappear into bottom sediment, casters do not. They lie there in full view on the bottom of the swim just waiting to be sucked up.

Water-borne baits

Caddis Grubs

Not only are larvae of the aquatic sedge flies, better known as caddis grubs, an important food source to cyprinids in both still and running water, they are an excellent natural bait which is entirely free.

There are nearly 200 different British species. Some are free-swimming, but most build portable homes 1–2 in long from sand and stone particles or pieces of wood, which they glue together. These cases offer the grub both home and protection while it crawls about on the bottom during the yearly cycle of metamorphosis starting with the egg laid by the adult fly, until the larva eventually pupates and moves up to the surface or the

31

The tools of the trade for collecting natural baits from brooks and side streams: a large holding bucket, complete with aerator; a one-gallon collecting tub with neck strap; nets various, including a really fine mesh aquarium net with a strong wire frame; and a wine bottle minnow trap. (See diagram on page 38)

shore, where the body splits open, enabling the fly to emerge.

To find a supply of baits takes but a few minutes of turning over rocks and large flints or fallen branches along the shallows. To remove the maggot-like grub from its home, simply pinch its tail while easing its head and legs out from the front with thumb and forefinger.

A size 14 hook holds one caddis grub perfectly for rudd, dace or roach, while two on a size 12 is ideal for bream and chub. Whether you wish to inject a little natural history into your sport, or have left the bait box on the garage floor miles away and urgently require bait, roll your sleeves up and start rummaging around in the shallows. You won't be disappointed.

Mayfly Nymphs

As most fly fishermen are aware, the beautiful mayfly, with its distinctive three long tails, is by far the largest of our upwinged flies. It is found in lakes, ponds and in both slow and fast-flowing rivers throughout the British Isles. Generally the yearly cycle of this fly culminates in the main hatch coming off some time between mid-May and mid-June. Therefore only during the early weeks of the coarse-fishing season will nymphs be available — because they are all about to hatch — to gather for hookbaits.

However, during the winter the eggs laid by the females in May and June will have matured into sizeable nymphs, larger than a caddis grub, particularly suitable for presenting on a size 14 hook when trotting for dace, roach or grayling. Collect

mayfly nymphs by sifting through fine gravel or silt close to reed or rush stems in the margins with a strong, fine-mesh aquarium net. They are a distinctive creamy colour with brown markings and, of course, three tails. Any other largish nymphs — those of the stone flies, for instance — can be used with equal effectiveness.

Bloodworms

Wherever you spot the feeding bubbles of tench or carp exploding in the surface film of still waters, it is odds-on they are syphoning through the bottom detritus for the little red bloodworm, the larva of the midge.

While there are hundreds of bloodworm variants, either living in the silt on the bottom of still waters, in plant tissue, in little tubes which they construct, or even swimming freely, it is the bright-red (because of the haemoglobin in the blood) segmented larva of some of the larger species which match fishermen, in particular, use for bait. Some species of midge have a yearly cycle like most other aquatic flies, while others produce two or three generations during a season. This makes them about the most prolific source of natural food to all bottom feeders, because the greater part of their cycle is spent in larval form and so they are always readily available, summer and winter.

Most cyprinids share a love of bloodworms (as do perch and ruffe) and in both clear and really cold water they are by far the most effective bait for smaller species such as gudgeon and roach. The trouble is, their size alone calls for a very delicate

The larvae of the sedge fly, better known as caddis grubs, are slightly larger than maggots, and are entirely free to gather. Relished by all cyprinid species, they are found in shallow water, clinging to the undersides of large flints, rocks and waterlogged branches in their portable home made from sand, shells and twigs.

33

presentation demanding the use of gossamer hooklengths and tiny, fine-wire hooks. The bloodworm is then best nicked gently through the darker, more bulbous head end so that it hangs straight.

Obtaining bloodworms yourself is a laborious, messy job requiring chest waders and the construction of a scraper for obtaining them from shallow, silty ponds and lakes. To a long broomstick add a 12 in length of flat-steel of around 1 in wide and $\frac{1}{16}$ in thick (see diagram). It should be set at a right angle so that when scraped just beneath the top layer of silt, where the greatest concentration of bloodworms live, they 'fold' and are held against the blade edge.

As you lift the scraper out of the water, a quick sideways turn of the wrist will ensure that the worms do not immediately fall off. Then tap the scraper on the side of a floating riddle or sieve, to knock off both debris and bloodworms. The worms crawl through the top riddle into the chamber below, leaving behind all the debris.

Much smaller species of midge, referred to as jokers and used purely as loose feed when bloodworms are presented on the hook, are most commonly found in semi-polluted streams, particularly below sewage outfalls. Collect them by disturbing the bottom sediment and netting them *en masse* in a large, extremely fine-mesh net when the float up. They can be separated from all the unwanted bits of weed and debris by putting the whole lot into a fine-weave sack and lowering it into a bucket of water, then waiting for the jokers to crawl through the mesh into clear water.

But the fact is, most of us just haven't the time for lengthy bait-collecting sessions, and the easiest way of obtaining bloodworms, if rather expensive — though now you know why — is by the pint from your nearest specialist tackle shop. To ensure bloodworms keep for as long as possible, put them in peat wrapped in newspaper and store them in the fridge.

Freshwater Shrimps

Several species of freshwater shrimps live in still and running water, on the bottom among rooted weedbeds, but I have always found the largest species in tidal rivers. Sifting along the bottom with a strong-framed, fine-mesh aquarium net will soon produce dozens and dozens of them from streams.

I have never found them to be an 'electric' bait, which is rather puzzling, given that all cyprinids eat shrimps. When they are presented one or two up on a size 14 hook and trotted downstream, the most likely customers are grayling, dace, roach and chub.

Sea Shrimps and Prawns

At exactly what size a sea shrimp becomes a prawn I am not sure. Let's call those under about 1 in shrimps and everything

Collecting blood-worms.

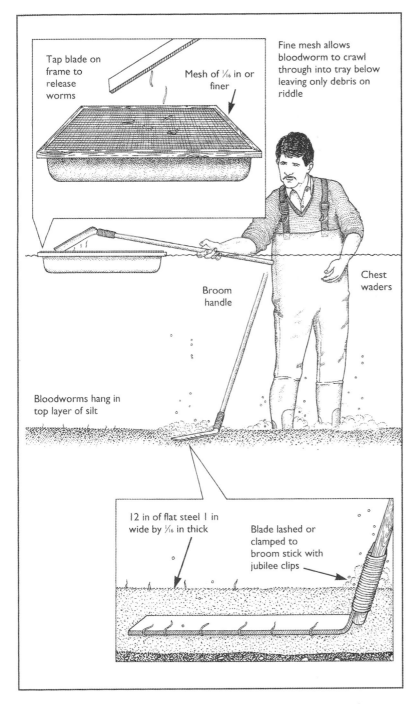

Tap blade on frame to release worms

Mesh of ⅟₁₆ in or finer

Fine mesh allows bloodworm to crawl through into tray below leaving only debris on riddle

Chest waders

Broom handle

Bloodworms hang in top layer of silt

12 in of flat steel 1 in wide by ⅟₁₆ in thick

Blade lashed or clamped to broom stick with jubilee clips

larger prawns. Not that it really matters, because it is best to gauge the size of the bait to the species expected.

Both are most economically bought from the fishmonger's slab either in their natural, translucent grey-green, uncooked state, or already boiled and peeled, which turns them pink. It makes good sense to buy both in bulk, divide them into batches and pop them into the freezer.

35

Peeled or unpeeled, and secured carefully through the tail end with a large-eyed hook tied direct, prawns attract chub, eels, perch, carp and barbel.

Natural shrimps and prawns do not look very different from the freshwater crayfish, which, I am convinced, is why they are relished by chub and barbel. Shrimps are ideal in size for long-trotting when presented on a size 8 hook, while a size 4 is none too large for freelining a prawn downstream through clear runs between long, flowing weedbeds or beneath rafts of weed and overhanging trees. In fast currents, pinch a swan shot or two 20 in above the prawn and at the end of the run gently retrieve it with irregular pulls and twitches. Chub, in particular, find this absolutely irresistible, although unfortunately so does the occasional pike.

If there is a problem with using ready-peeled and boiled shrimps and prawns, it is that you end up eating most of them yourself, so do take enough. River fish such as chub and barbel invariably respond quickly to a few loose offerings scattered into the head of the swim, whereas stillwater species usually require a few prebaiting sessions in order to acquire a taste. I have enjoyed most success with tench and carp (although I have never tried them for bream) when float fishing, because the meat of ready-boiled shrimps and prawns is rather soft and the hook can pull out if you leger at distance. So consider them a close-range bait. Freelining a couple of large, peeled prawns on a size 4 hook provides a good mouthful, not only for carp but for catfish and eels too.

Crayfish

This mini lobster is by far our largest crustacean and freshwater invertebrate. It leads a mainly nocturnal life, feeding on small dead or dying fish, shrimps, snails and insects, resting during daylight beneath rocks, large flints, sunken logs and in holes in the clay banks of clear-flowing streams and rivers. It thrives well in limestone districts, and the fast-flowing chalkstreams of southern England, which have the high calcium content so necessary for hardening its shell (like crabs and lobsters, the crayfish must discard its old shell and harden new skin into shell to grow larger) were once full of crayfish. Indeed, so were many stream-fed lakes and gravel pits, but sadly this is no longer the case.

As more and more of our streams and rivers suffer through chronic abstraction and an oxygen deficiency caused by pollutants such as human sewage effluent, both treated and untreated, pig slurry, silage, and concentrated farming chemicals, the crayfish is always one of the first creatures to go. It is the best guide to a river's purity and health, and its decline does not figure in the publicity reports and complicated graphs showing commercial gain which water companies love to issue to their shareholders.

Fished throughout the summer and autumn in the same way as a slug, simply freelined through the swim on 6-lb line with a size 6 or 4 hook nicked through the last tail segment, the cray-

Hooked gently through the top lip or through both nostrils, a minnow will catch perch and chub whether freelined or trotted through clear runs between weedbeds. To catch barbel, tap the minnow on the head and then leger it.

37

Wine bottle minnow trap.

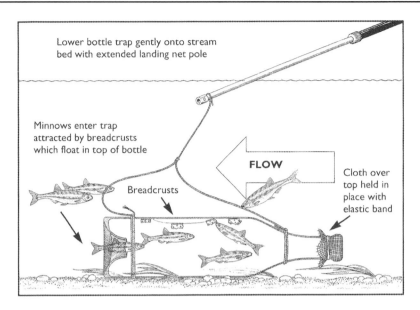

Lower bottle trap gently onto stream bed with extended landing net pole

Minnows enter trap attracted by breadcrusts which float in top of bottle

FLOW

Breadcrusts

Cloth over top held in place with elastic band

fish will draw the craftiest chub from its lie and produce the most positive, slamming bite. And, of course, since the crayfish swims backwards, which is its defence when you try to pick one up, chub are just as likely to grab hold on the retrieve. Pike, perch, trout and barbel love them and so do jack pike.

I would dearly love to write much more about this fascinating creature, which abounded in the streams of Hertfordshire where most of my teenage fishing took place. There I spent as much time learning about creatures on the bottom of the river as I did fishing with the natural baits I collected. However, the demise of our rivers prompts me instead to suggest that, should you be fortunate enough to find a crayfish, far more a river still prolific with them, you treat the event as a privilege and opt for another chub bait. This chapter is full of them.

Minnows

Swatting a fine-mesh landing net down quickly on the surface of a shallow stream, having first attracted a shoal of minnows with a little mashed bread or dry crumb groundbait, and sweeping it out again with equal speed, is one way of gathering these tiddlers for use as bait. Alternatively, you can catch them easily enough using a size 20 hook baited with a small maggot, preferably a pinkie or a squatt. It is fair to say that in some rivers minnows are a confounded nuisance to anglers long-trotting maggots for roach, dace and chub during the summer. How these small-mouthed scavengers actually manage two maggots on a size 14 hook (never when you want to catch them, though) amazes me, but where competition is fierce they seem to have little trouble.

There is a third and traditional method of obtaining minnows: using a trap made from a clear-glass wine or champagne bottle (see diagram). Choose one with an inverted funnel at the base, fill it with earth or sand and then push it into earth or sand until the base is level and everything is packed tight. By carefully tapping at the centre of the funnel — use a short piece of ½-in dowel and a hammer — you will knock out a neat hole through which the minnows will pass into the bottle when it is lowered, the neck facing upstream, on to the river bed.

It is wise to have several suitable bottles to hand as glass does not always break as planned. Over the bottle's neck fix a piece of cloth with an elastic band and after popping a few crusts of bread inside through the bottom, tie on a cord connected at both ends so that the trap can be lowered gently on the end of your extended landing-net handle.

Trapping minnows can be great fun and helps to bring back some of those boyhood memories when even the smallest fish raised the adrenalin level. And as a bait for perch, eels, chub and barbel 'minners are winners'. Having caught a batch, keep them in a gallon-sized maggot bucket in no more than 1 in of water. The continual sloshing around as you walk will help to oxygenate the water.

Minnows are best hooked once only through the top lip or through both nostrils with a hook of size 8 to 4 (depending on the size of the minnow) tied direct to a 5 or 6-lb line. You can freeline them beneath overhanging bushes or weed rafts to chub, retrieving them in an erratic twitch-and-pause motion. Or they can be trotted down through clear runs between thick weedbeds, supported by a chunky 'chubber' or 'loafer' float, slightly undershotted to compensate for the minnow's weight. During the early season, especially when fry shoals of all species are a readily available food source, minnows are a deadly bait for barbel.

In slow swims, pinch on a swan shot or two to hold the minnow down on the bottom, or for tackling deep, fast runs close into the bank, weir pools and similar situations, anchor it down using a running bomb stopped 8 in from the hook.

Where perch are expected in deep holes on the bends, trot minnows slowly along with the float set to present the bait 18 in off the bottom. Or set up a mini float-paternoster rig using two size 12 swivels with a bomb heavy enough to keep the rig in the desired spot until a perch grabs it (see diagram).

Stone Loach

Apart from intentionally catching stone loach on float-fished worm fragments and tiny hooks from the local brook when a boy, I can only ever remember catching one on rod and line since then. This is strange, because they are prolific in most small, clear-flowing streams throughout the British Isles and make an extremely robust bait (even when repeatedly cast) with a great attraction for eels, perch, chub and barbel.

39

Right: Float paternoster rig for perch using minnows in deep holes on the bends of rivers.

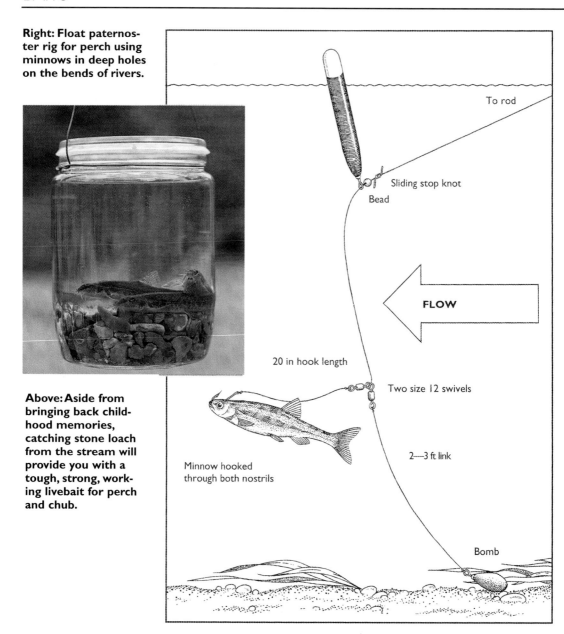

To rod

Sliding stop knot

Bead

FLOW

20 in hook length

Two size 12 swivels

Above: Aside from bringing back child-hood memories, catching stone loach from the stream will provide you with a tough, strong, working livebait for perch and chub.

Minnow hooked through both nostrils

2–3 ft link

Bomb

There is also another smaller, much rarer loach — the spined loach — which lives in just a few counties in England. You could be excused initially for mistaking a stone loach, which grows to 4 in, for a baby barbel. But a close look reveals four whiskers on the barbel and no fewer than six on the stone loach.

To collect this lively, yellowy-brown-mottled fish search the shallows by placing a rectangular, fine-mesh aquarium net hard against the bottom in an upright position immediately down-stream of any large stone, house brick, or the like, which should be gently eased up and moved to one side. This washes

If you want an entirely free, easy to gather, natural bait for tench, carp, eels and catfish, look no further than the humble swan mussel. John's son Lee uses a garden rake to collect these from around the margins of gravel pits.

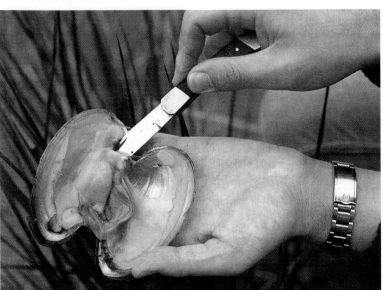

Severing the hinges of a mussel with a fine-bladed knife will reveal the orangy meat inside. Offer the entire chunk on a large hook tied direct, throwing in several loose pieces as groundbait.

41

anything beneath the hide-out into the net. Always replace the stone in exactly the same position afterwards.

Use a size 6 or 4 hook (depending on the bait's size) tied directly to 6-lb line, and gently sleeve the point through both nostrils. Loach can be freelined, trotted, legered or float-paternostered a couple of feet above the bottom, just like minnows. They are a super perch bait for use in deep gravel pits where, regardless of depth, they will work attractively.

Bullheads

When flushing out stone loach from beneath the larger rocks on the bottom of streams, you cannot help but catch bullheads or, as they are often nicknamed, on account of their distinctive flattened head, miller's thumbs. They may be fished in exactly the same way as loach and minnows, but are generally not as effective. When freelining for chub, tap the bullhead on the head before casting, or it will zoom straight down to the bottom into a hidey-hole.

Brook Lampreys

These curious, primitive, eel-like fishes, equipped with a circular, sucking mouth, adhere to the undersides of large stones, and even when adult rarely attain more than 6 in. They are quick off the mark when disturbed, but can be caught in an aquarium net like all other small fishes living in clear-flowing streams.

In the infant stage they live a semi-dormant existence, blind, toothless and yellow-buff in colour, buried in soft silt or mud beneath tree roots on the inside of acute bends, where silt beds accumulate, and in the build-up of silt and debris behind bridge supports.

Adult brook lampreys are heavy enough to be freelined, and a simply electric bait for chub. Hook them once only through the mouth with a size 6 hook tied direct to 5 or 6-lb line, and retrieve the bait in jerks and twitches if nothing grabs hold on the way through the swim. Infant brook lampreys work well when trotted beneath a chunky float, being readily taken by both perch and chub, and no doubt a barbel would not refuse one legered. It is a natural bait which is as interesting to collect as it is to use.

Elvers

Baby eels, or elvers, which run up our rivers during the summer after their arduous journey from the Sargasso Sea, are consumed in vast quantities by trout, sea trout, pike, perch, chub and barbel. As they are extremely thin, almost transparent and just 3–4 in long, take great care when hooking them on. Nick a size 8 or 6 hook gently through the head or middle, and either freeline two at close range or trot one downstream beneath a chunky float.

Elvers are best collected at night with a net (a micromesh landing net is perfect). With a powerful torch, look on the surface around the sluices of weir and mill pools, where elvers collect in their thousands during their up-river migration.

Mussels

Mussels are found on the bottom of most rivers and lakes. There are several British species, ranging in size from the tiny pea mussel to the huge swan mussel, which can measure up to 10 in in length. They often live with their shells part buried, breathing and feeding by syphoning water through their system, and will survive happily in a bucket of water for several days. The orange meat inside a swan mussel is relished by bream, tench, carp, eels and catfish.

To collect mussels drag a long-handled garden rake slowly along the bottom of any lake or gravel pit. If the silt is too deep for raking, roll your sleeves up and simply feel for them. Use a thin-bladed knife to open the shell by severing the muscles either side of the hinge. Present the large piece of orange flesh on hooks, tied direct to the reel line, of sizes 6 to 2, depending on the size of the mussel, and use simple freeline tactics. Throw in the loose pieces for groundbait. For catfish increase the hook size to 1/0. To almost guarantee hectic action with tench, eels or carp, prebait a swim every other day for a week with the insides of 10–20 mussels. But don't take my word for it — try them yourself.

Cockles

Like shrimps and prawns, cockles are best purchased in bulk, ready-shelled and boiled, from the fishmonger's, and then split up into batches and popped straight into the freezer in polythene bags.

This most effective and convenient bait, which attracts tench, carp, eels, catfish, chub, barbel and carp, may even be coloured before freezing. For a pint of cockles, simply add a teaspoon of powder carp-bait dye to a cupful of boiling water and swish the cockles around in a two-pint bait box for a few minutes before straining off the excess fluid and bagging up the cockles. Yellow, orange and deep red all look quite startling, but whether you are using coloured or plain cockles, scatter a handful into the swim (or many swims) for several consecutive days before fishing with them.

Cockles may be freelined — three or four on a size 4 hook provides enough weight — legered, or presented lift-style beneath a length of peacock quill. While cockles initially seem rather alien, being a sea creature, they do look remarkably like the insides of a small mussel — a fact which most freshwater species quickly switch on to.

43

Whether coloured (use powder carp bait dye) or plain, boiled cockles are a fabulous natural bait for many summer species, whether float-fished, legered or freelined.

Squid

Continuing on the 'sea bait' theme, with its unique smell and firm flesh the squid, or calamari as it is widely known, is a great natural bait for several freshwater species. Eels accept it readily, but the squid is perhaps best known as *the* bait for luring catfish.

I prefer small, whole squid of 4–6 in long, which marry nicely with a large hook of size 2 to 1/0. To prevent a fold of rubbery skin masking the point of the hook on the strike, I rig a tiny 'holding' hook 2 in up the trace to keep the bait straight and stop it nudging down (see diagram). This works effectively whether you are offering a whole baby squid or a strip cut lengthways from the body of a large squid.

A point well worth mentioning here is that the syndicate members who fish for catfish in my two carp fisheries catch far more carp than catfish. Therefore I urge you to try squid wher-

Presenting squid.

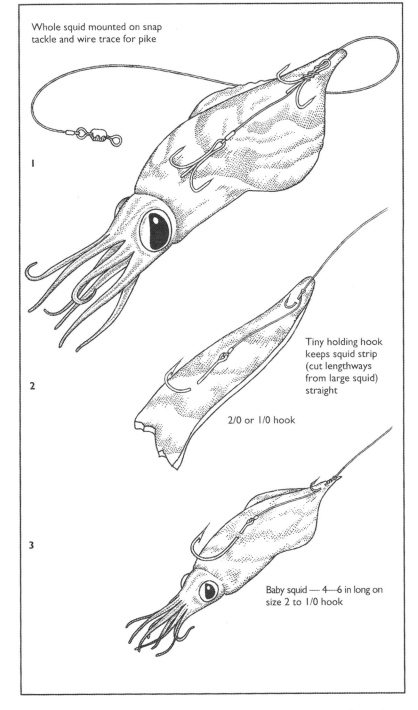

Whole squid mounted on snap tackle and wire trace for pike

1

2

Tiny holding hook keeps squid strip (cut lengthways from large squid) straight

2/0 or 1/0 hook

3

Baby squid — 4—6 in long on size 2 to 1/0 hook

ever you seek carp in heavily coloured waters or at night, when their powers of smell are put on maximum alert. It can prove devastating. Pike also gobble up squid (see Deadbaits, page 115).

Buy squid fresh from the market and pop it straight into the

45

freezer individually wrapped in clingfilm or a polythene bag if it is not to be used immediately.

Whitebait

Although a handful of whitebait scattered around a static dead-bait increases its attraction for approaching perch, catfish, eels, zander and pike (whitebait are good for prebaiting too, because they do not 'overfeed') I have included this tiny sardine among natural baits. It is readily available from most wet-fish shops, delicatessens and in frozen packs from large supermarkets, and especially during the autumn and winter, is a prime, reasonably selective bait for attracting stillwater chub.

The regular prebaiting of marginal swims just as darkness falls — any earlier only attracts diving birds — has the effect of initiating a 'feeding route' which chub soon follow every evening.

Present two whitebait on a size 4 or 2 hook tied to a Dacron hooklength (to avoid possible bite-offs from the chub's power-ful pharyngeal teeth) and either light leger or freeline. Watch out for pike and eels, though, and carp.

Mashed, minced or liquidized, whitebait added to brown breadcrumbs makes a superb groundbait for any of the species mentioned above.

CHAPTER TWO

MANUFACTURED BAITS

Bread

Breadflake

Because the polythene bag encourages moisture, which makes the bread last longer, I much prefer to buy ready-sliced white loaves. And to ensure breadflake stays on and you are not simply sitting there with a bare hook, insist on fresh, doughy white bread. If you shop around and try various brands you will no doubt notice a difference between loaves. As second choice, a large, freshly baked tin loaf makes good breadflake. Either way, it pays to keep one or two loaves in reserve in the freezer just in case.

In addition to using only the fresh, doughy white bread of a new loaf, the secret of ensuring that flake stays on the hook is to compress it really hard between thumb and forefinger around the shank of the hook while masking the point and barb with the other thumb. It then swells to twice the size when it becomes wet, with an attractive, fluffy (unpressed) part hiding the hook point, which easily finds a purchase on the strike.

I rate breadflake among the better standard baits for good-sized dace, rudd, roach, bream and tench, whether freelined, presented 'on the lift' or legered. A lump of flake the size of a 2p piece, for instance, hiding a size 8 or 6 hook, will, because of its size, put you straight through a shoal of rudd or roach of mixed sizes to the whoppers.

A cocktail of flake on the hook shank, with either maggot, corn, caster, wheat or worm on the bend, provides yet another trick up your sleeve when fish are wary. A balanced bait (excellent for presenting over thick bottom weed) of crust on the shank with a pinch of flake round the bend is also worth trying.

Breadcrust

Although the crust has nowhere near the durability of breadflake as far as staying on the hook is concerned, because

47

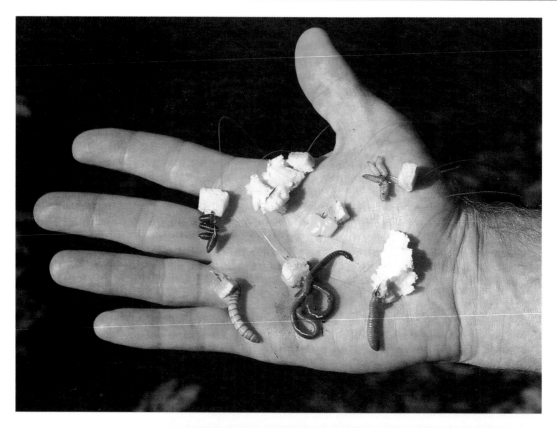

Above: As a change bait from using plain bread on the hook, why not try flake or crust cocktails. Sometimes that little extra difference can really switch spooky fish on — especially bream, rudd and tench.

Right: Though considered by many as 'old hat' bait, breadcrust can still tempt carp. This beautiful orange koi accepted a small cube of brown breadcrust freelined into a tiny gap in a large bed of lilies.

48

This 15 lb-plus Asiatic grass carp is a comparative rarity in British waters, but it fell for a standard ploy. John tempted it on a tiny balanced crust and breadflake combination, presented on a size 12 hook tied direct to 6-lb test in conjunction with a tenpin floating controller.

of its buoyancy, presenting a cube of crust on the hook often scores over most other baits. A situation which immediately springs to mind is legering or float-fishing over a weedy or debris-covered bottom. This applies not only to stillwaters but also to long-trotting in swift-flowing rivers for roach, chub or barbel. Bear in mind that crust swells to around twice its size when saturated, and cut the cubes accordingly.

If you are using reasonably small hooks, say size 16 to 10, then the crust from the edge of a sliced white loaf is perfect. Large hooks demand bigger crusts and then I much prefer to buy small tin loaves because there is little white bread wastage once the crusts have been removed. I also like the rubbery crust of a fresh — and I stress 'fresh' — French loaf. Again, because the loaf is narrow, not much white bread is wasted.

49

Presenting floaters.

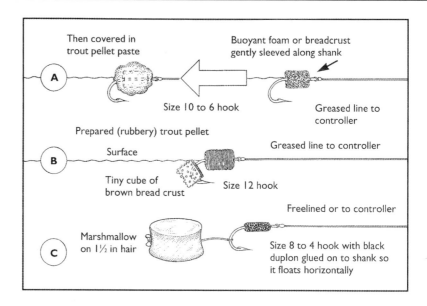

Then covered in trout pellet paste

Buoyant foam or breadcrust gently sleeved along shank

A

Size 10 to 6 hook

Greased line to controller

Prepared (rubbery) trout pellet

Surface

Greased line to controller

B

Tiny cube of brown bread crust

Size 12 hook

Freelined or to controller

Marshmallow on 1½ in hair

C

Size 8 to 4 hook with black duplon glued on to shank so it floats horizontally

As with flake, crust cocktails are very effective, particularly for presenting 'on the drop'. Try an oblong of crust on the hook shank, with a maggot, caster, corn, worm or even a piece of flake on the bend, for a truly balanced bait. A balanced crust and flake trick, which carp fall for time and time again if they are attracted by surface crusts, is to slide a small piece of crust up over the eye of the hook, then squeeze on a large piece of breadflake, which, if presented on its own, would immediately start to sink. However, if you gently pinch a corner of the flake together with the white bread on the crust, the crust holds the flake until a carp inspects the bait, knocking it with its lips, the top of its head, or even with a swish of the tail, as carp often do.

Once separated, the waterlogged flake suddenly starts to sink, and wham, the carp sucks it in greedily with complete confidence because it is behaving naturally. Great fun.

At close range, use simple freeline tactics (remember to grease the line) and for distances in excess of 20 yards, use the added weight of a small floating controller such as a tenpin to place the crust or crust and flake combination accurately (see diagram).

Breadpaste (see page55)

Punched Bread

When a fish's metabolism slows right down and conditions are difficult — the water is clear or cold or both — offering a tiny pellet of punched bread on the hook is an excellent alternative to maggots or casters. Dace, rudd and roach, in particular, readily respond to it.

Use a really fresh, sliced white loaf and rest a slice on a hard

50

board so that a neat pellet is formed when you press the punch into it.

Making Your Own Coloured Bread

If the situation arises, as it does in carp fishing for instance, where fish quickly wise up to bread and particularly its stark whiteness, one answer is to change the bait's colour. This occurred to me many years ago and I have since had considerable success when, for instance, surface fishing 'black' breadcrust. This has nowhere near the shock effect on carp that have previously succumbed too many times to crust from an untreated white loaf.

Black breadflake, orange breadflake, pink breadflake and so on may sound strange, but do give them a try, and you will find other species, such as tench, bream and chub, will also respond favourably.

To make your own 2lb loaf exactly the colour of your choice could not be easier. You will need a 1¼-lb packet of white bread mix, powder colouring, hot water and an appropriately sized baking tin.

First dissolve a level teaspoon of powder colouring (two spoonfuls of black) into ¾ pint of hand-hot water. Then put the bread mix in a large bowl and slowly add the coloured water, stirring thoroughly. Knead the dough with your hands for a timed five minutes, and then place it in the baking tin, which should be slightly greased and floured. Put clingfilm over the tin and leave it in a warm place for half an hour until the dough doubles in size.

Place the tin in the middle of a preheated oven set on gas mark 8 (230°C) for 45 minutes. And hey presto, your very own loaf in exactly the colour you want.

Groundbaits

Mashed Bread

Hanging from a nail in my garage (so that the mice cannot reach it) is an old keepnet full of dried bread scraps, which I use to make mashed-bread groundbait. To stop bread scraps from going mouldy, pop a batch in the oven on a large tray for a few minutes.

The secret of making mashed-bread groundbait is to use stale bread at least five or six days old. While it really doesn't matter how old the bread is, never use new bread. Start by soaking a batch of scraps in a bucket of water for a couple of hours and then straining off the excess water, before squeezing and mashing the bread between your fingers into a fine pulp. The success of mashed bread can be attributed to its make-up of thousands of tiny, separate, fluffy particles which attract more than they overfeed.

51

Whether dyed black or orange, coloured bread provides a most interesting and effective change bait to surface feeders like rudd, chub and particularly carp. And it is so easy to make.

When you are using mashed bread during the winter in running water, for instance, if it is not quickly eaten, the cloud of mash soon passes on downstream through the swim and disintegrates without overfeeding the intended quarry of quality roach or chub. By the way, rather than freeze my hands off squeezing out mash in sub-zero temperatures at the river, I make it up in the kitchen sink in warm water the night before an early-morning stint, and after squeezing out the excess water pop it into a polythene bag.

Alternatively, if you store bags of ready-made and squeezed mash in the freezer, just take one out and leave it in the sink overnight so that by dawn it will have defrosted sufficiently for throwing in. Immediately before baiting up I like to squeeze the mash again into golf balls, and the tighter it is squeezed the longer it holds together before breaking up.

To obtain a nice 'cloud' for use with, say, punched bread, make your mash sloppy and squeeze it into tiny balls. But if you are seeking bream, which form huge shoals, stiffen a sloppy mash with bran, maize meal, dry breadcrumbs or even a proprietary groundbait, plus hookbait fragments of corn, worms, casters or wheat, and so on (if you are not using flake or paste as hookbait) and mould it into firm cricket balls. In really deep, fast rivers, the best binders for mashed bread are flaked maize, which looks like heavy-duty cornflakes (you can use ordinary cornflakes) and pearl barley. Both help take your mash straight down to the bottom, regardless of depth.

Breadcrumbs

Breadcrumbs, plus additives such as crushed hempseed or maize meal, are the universal base for most prepacked 'special' groundbaits. But you can easily make your own from crunching up toasted bread scraps kept in an old keepnet, as I do, or buy plain brown or white breadcrumbs in 2 or 3-lb bags, or in bulk, which is by far the cheapest way.

To dampened crumbs various binders may be added. For bream fishing in deep, fast rivers and in stillwaters where you want the bait to go straight to the bottom, add either pearl barley or flaked maize, plus hookbait samples. Whether using them on the hook or not, casters are a most valuable inclusion, and far better than maggots, which tend to wriggle and break up the ball even before it is thrown, and then quickly disappear into the bottom sediment if not eaten immediately. By contrast, casters lay there on the bottom in full view among the cereal carpet and make nice firm balls for throwing or catapulting.

Incidentally, if your maggots turn into 'floating' casters, don't throw them away in disgust, whatever the amount. For adding to breadcrumbs, there is nothing more attractive. With your fingers, crush a handful at a time into a pulp over the tub of crumbs, so that the juices and the millions of shell fragments all go in. Add a little water if necessary, and the resulting 'cloud' from the casters' juices creates a mix to which bream respond eagerly. It is particularly effective in lakes and canals which are difficult because of their clear water.

Above left: Dried breadscraps, which are thoroughtly soaked and then squeezed into a mash, are a superb groundbait for chub and bream. To stiffen this mash for throwing long distances, and so it sinks quickly through fast, deep water down to the bottom, various ingredients must be added.

Above right: For species like bream, aim to prebait as dusk falls on the evening prior to the morning's fishing (unless you intend fishing throughout the night) so that water birds and other anglers do not show interest in your chosen swim.

53

When tench fishing, I add to the breadcrumbs a pint of fine, granulated trout-pellet feed or salmon fry crumbs plus, when obtainable, a pint of fresh blood from the butcher's. Crushed hempseed is another excellent additive. I also mix in a few hookbait samples such as corn, casters, chopped worms or maggots.

To make a much lighter breadcrumb groundbait for rudd, roach and bream hybrids, use fine breadcrumbs and mix them in a shallow bowl or tray by fluffing the crumbs about with your free hand while trickling in water from a spare bait box with the other. To ensure the mix will break up quickly into a cloud, or will go straight down when squeezed tightly, put it through an $\frac{1}{8}$-in riddle to eradicate any hard, stodgy lumps. Finally, add a handful of the hookbait.

For feeder fishing with either plastic open-ended or metal-cage feeders, I prefer really coarse breadcrumbs since these, if only lightly dampened, hold together well yet explode instantly the feeder touches bottom. When using plastic open-ended feeders, it is a simple matter to fill the middle with hookbait fragments and plug each end with slightly dampened coarse crumbs.

Prebaiting and Swim Clearance

Simply heaving in a bucketful of free nosh is not always the key to instant success. It will undoubtedly make shoal fish, bream in particular, congregate within a chosen area, following several days of prebaiting wherever shoals are large, but there are side-effects to consider. For instance, try to prebait only as dusk falls, since this not only coincides with a part of the day when bream feed more aggressively, but will also attract the attention of neither waterfowl such as swans, mallards and coots, nor opportunist anglers who could very well reap the rewards of your efforts.

While prebaiting is going on, it pays to visit in the morning to look for visual signs of bream activity in the swim: streams of bubbles, heavily discoloured water or rolling bream. If the swim is in a distant area reachable only by boat or a long walk, then take your binoculars. Whether prebaiting, fish spotting or actually fishing, I never leave mine at home.

In flowing water that is really heavily populated with bream — for instance, many rivers in Denmark and Ireland — a good helping of groundbait at dusk is invariably enough to ensure hectic sport at dawn. But the bream in huge stillwater fisheries are known to take their time, especially in summer, when pickings are rich, and so prebaiting for two or three days could be useful.

Much of the above also applies to tench, which likewise respond to a good stirring up of the bottom and actual weed clearance before the bait is presented. I have even caught good-sized tench while a friend has been in the process of throwing out a heavy weed rake. Tench rarely seem perturbed about the commotion; on the contrary, I'm certain it attracts them. Once they locate the disturbed bottom silt with the mountain of tiny, natural items of food it contains in suspension, plus fragments of your hookbaits and cereal base, they might well root about in the swim for several hours.

Pastes

Breadpaste

Plain breadpaste is a bait I often use in preference to breadflake on the hook when bream fishing. They hang on to paste just that much longer in order for a strike to be made before the bait disintegrates. For the same reason, although to a much lesser extent, plain white breadpaste also works effectively with quality dace, rudd and roach. Tench and chub too succumb to paste when it is used in conjunction with mashed-bread groundbait.

To make a super creamy breadpaste simply soak several slices of four to five day-old bread (or a chunk from a tin loaf with the crust removed) under the cold tap and knead it with clean hands until it reaches a firm consistency. Like cheese paste, it can be frozen for future use.

Cat-food Paste

Just about every brand of tinned cat food will, if sufficiently stiffened, make an excellent paste for tench, carp and catfish. Most chub won't refuse it either.

The secret is to bind the paste together so that it does not break up on the hook. Mix it with cornflour (or plain flour) and wheatgerm (or Beemax) until it is firm. Wheat gluten, boilie gel and egg albumen are also binders well worth trying, with a sticky base, so experiment until a lump of paste will stay on the hook in a bucket of water for at least 20 minutes without disintegrating. A spoonful of powder colouring may also be kneaded in.

Cheese Paste

To make a cheese paste that will not go rock-hard in cold water and possibly impair hook preparation, simply mix together equal parts of finely grated Cheddar (Danish blue or Gorgonzola if your prefer, and can handle the pong) and mashed bread. Start by soaking under the cold tap several slices of white bread or a chunk (with the crust removed) from a tin loaf. Bread at least four or five days old is best and should be kneaded until creamy. Now add the grated cheese and continue kneading the mix until it is of a fairly stiff consistency. I don't think adding colour is necessary, but any powder dye

55

When filling a plastic
open-ended feeder or
wire mesh-cage
feeder with
breadcrumbs, do not
overwet, or they will
clog together and not
explode and disperse
instantly on impact
with the bottom.

When bream show a
reluctance for plain
breadflake, Terry
Smith tempts them
with a hookbait of
soft, creamy
breadpaste, used in
conjunction with
slightly dampened
white breadcrumbs
packed into an open-
ended feeder.

56

If you are a chub addict, then it is well worth taking the time to ensure your cheesepaste is of a smooth consistency without any nasty lumps to impair hook penetration on the strike.

may be added and kneaded in at almost any stage. To simply intensify the yellow, add a teaspoonful of turmeric.

Cheese paste is a superb bait for chub, barbel, carp and even tench. It can easily be spiced up a little once carp, for instance, start to wise up to the basic cheese and bread base, by adding a teaspoon of either Marmite, Bovril, curry powder or Phillips' yeast mixture, which is a cage-bird tonic that really pongs. For immediate use, wrap the ball of paste in a square of clean cloth, or put it into a polythene bag and freeze it until needed.

Flour and Water Paste

During my childhood immediately after the Second World War, fancy adhesives for sticking cuttings and pictures into scrapbooks were not available, and so everyone used a runny paste made from flour and water. It is the natural gluten in flour which binds a simple flour and water paste together and stops it coming off the hook. So if you suddenly find yourself without a loaf of bread in the cupboard or freezer, don't despair. There is bound to be a bag of flour in the kitchen.

Put three cupfuls of flour into a bowl and slowly add cold water while stirring briskly with a spoon until the mix is of a firm enough consistency for kneading. Although well-kneaded

57

plain white dough will readily catch roach, bream, tench, chub and carp, you can spice it up by adding a large spoonful of either custard or blancmange powder to the flour before adding water. This results in a large ball of bright-yellow or pink (pink is the best of the blancmange colours) paste with a really distinctive aroma.

Ragi Paste

I was first introduced to this superb bait in the 1980s when fishing for the mighty mahseer in India. It is probably fair to state that more mahseer are caught on ragi — spinners, spoons, livebaits and deadbaits are also taken — than on any other bait or lure. The reason for this is simple. Once properly prepared, ragi, which is made from the flour of millet, will stay on the hook in the fastest currents (unless pecked by tiddlers) where the mahseer lives, certainly for up to half an hour. I have timed this.

It is ironic that while we all tend to think of boilies as a recent invention created for carp, history books reveal that balls of boiled ragi — boilies, no less — were used to catch mahseer well over a century ago.

The ragi flour I used in India is grey but, when boiled, turns dark brown. Unfortunately I have not been able to obtain it in the UK (although there must be a specialist Indian-food supplier who stocks it) so I make do with millet flakes from the local wholefood shop. These I grind down in a mortar and pestle into a fine flour, and then mix with water to form a soft paste (with a teaspoon of brown powder dye to darken) and a pinch each of cumin and asafoetida (a garlic-like spice). I then mould the mix into balls the size of a chicken egg. These are placed in a saucepan of boiling water for 20–25 minutes, which brings out the natural gluten in the millet flour, making the balls decidedly rubbery. Afterwards they are laid out on a cloth to cool.

These large individual baits are geared to the size of the mahseer's mouth, so either break them up into smaller eggs and rework them before using as a rubbery paste or, from the start, roll the ragi paste into ½ or ¾-in boilies and boil these in batches, leaving them to cool for an hour afterwards. As they are small, reduce the boiling time to 5 minutes. Millet or ragi boilies can be presented on a hair rig in the normal manner. Whether you use ragi as a paste or as small boilies, it is a great carp bait that will also catch tench, and making it is well worth the effort.

Sadza Paste

'Sadza' is a word used for white maize meal throughout southern central Africa, where it is a valuable staple food. It is also the main constituent of a rubbery paste bait concocted especially for cyprinid type African freshwater species, including carp. I first used it to good effect at the Mazoe Dam near Harare in Zimbabwe, and have since tried it on my local Norfolk carp waters, substituting yellow for white maize meal. This is available from any corn merchant or the majority of tackle shops, who now add it to their maggots to stop them from sweating, in preference to sawdust.

To make a coconut-sized ball of sadza, add to 1½ pints of boiling water three cups of maize meal, one cup of plain white flour, two eggs and your choice of colouring and flavouring. Reduce the heat to a slow boil and work the mix firmly with a long wooden spoon until the ingredients form a rubbery paste. This takes only a couple of minutes. Remove the mix from the saucepan and put it into a plastic tub or bait box. Once it has cooled, it is ready for use after just a little extra moulding. Africans add a teaspoon each of curry powder and turmeric to the mix when seeking carp, or custard powder for bream. Experiment with various concoctions: caramel with orange powder dye, for instance, butterscotch and brown, or strawberry and red. Even without any colouring, sadza ends up a pale-yellow, extremely dense paste which stays on the hook much longer than plain breadpaste, and is ideal for roach, carp, rudd, tench and bream. It is a most effective bait, as well as inexpensive and very quick to make.

Sausage-meat Paste

For chub, barbel, tench and carp, sausage-meat makes a great, easily prepared paste bait. As a base, you have the choice of beef or pork sausage meat, both readily available from your local butcher or supermarket. Plain sausage-meat on its own is far too sticky and so cornflour (plain flour will do) should be kneaded in until it forms a smooth, pliable paste. This can be used either as loose offerings or as hookbait.

If the finished result is too pale in colour for your liking — in clear water carp do spook at light baits lying on a dark bottom — a teaspoon of dark powder colouring should be kneaded in before the flour. At the same time extra flavouring may also be added, in the form of a crumbled Oxo cube, a teaspoon of coriander or turmeric, ginger and so on — the possibilities are endless.

Sausage-meat paste, like all pastes, can be stored in the freezer.

Semolina Paste

When you are raiding the kitchen cupboard for potential paste ingredients, look out for semolina. Made from hard wheat and the starchy part before it is finely milled into flour, semolina is already widely used by many bait companies as a bulk ingredient in their boilie mixes. But is also makes a fine,

59

All large cyprinids — roach, rudd, tench, chub, barbel and above all carp — love pastes. This collection includes trout-pellet paste, cheesepaste, sadza paste, a Robin Red based protein paste, a soft milk protein paste, coloured sausage-meat paste and ragi paste.

rubbery paste that will actually stay on the hook for up to an hour. Honestly! I've timed it.

As the paste is rather light in colour, it is advisable to add powder colouring (and flavouring) to the semolina while in its dry state. Mixing could then not be quicker or easier. You simply add two cupfuls of semolina to a large saucepan containing two cupfuls of water which has been brought to the boil. Stir the mix firmly and quickly for 20–30 seconds and it is done. Transfer the coconut-sized ball of paste to a plate and allow it to cool for 20 minutes, then knead it into shape.

Give this bait a try for tench, chub and, of course, carp, varying the colour and flavour accordingly. Being dense and thus heavy, it is great for underarm freelining into lily pads and beneath overhanging willows.

Sluis Bird-food Pastes

Containing various cereals, milk and milk derivatives, seeds, vitamins, oils, fats, minerals, vegetables as well as meat and animal derivatives, these complete bird foods make fine baits for species such as tench and carp. They are available in bulk or prepacked in 100-gm bags from the local pet shop and are easy to mix into paste.

I use Sluis mynah food, a fairly coarse mix (which benefits from the removal of any raisins) and Sluis CLO, a much finer food and conditioner blended specifically for canaries and other cage-birds. Both are mixed in exactly the same way. Empty two cupfuls of either into a mixing bowl, together with three raw eggs (as a binder) and work the mix briskly into a creamy paste. Then simply add a teaspoon of powder dye if you wish to alter the colour from an attractive golden yellow with dark flecks. If you fancy giving the paste extra 'bite', add a tablespoon of Phillips' yeast mixture.

Soft Protein Pastes

If your recipes for making boilies include milk derivatives, and most do, then you will be pleased to know that simply mixing these in dry form with powder colour plus water to which a teaspoon of flavouring has been added, will make a super rubbery paste bait for carp and tench. Boilies, with their rubbery skin, were invented to thwart the attentions of small shoal fish, but in fisheries not plagued by bait-peckers soft pastes really are worth a try, especially where the inhabitants are continually bombarded with boilies.

A piece the size of a 50p coin hiding a size 6 or 4 hook is heavy enough to be accurately freelined, and flattened, it will free-fall slowly among soft weeds and lily pads without being hidden from view. You can even dictate the paste's buoyancy by ensuring that there are a couple of ounces of sodium caseinate in the mix. An effective formula is to mix in dry form equal parts of calcium caseinate, wheatgerm and soya isolate or semolina together with powder colouring. This you can store mixed in bulk in an airtight tub and turn into paste simply by adding water and kneading. Remember to add your liquid flavouring to the water immediately before mixing. It is also worth mentioning that to match the colour of the paste with that of the bottom (starkly contrasting baits scare carp), it is a good idea to make the paste darker than would appear necessary.

Commercial fish foods such as trout pellets, whether sinkers or floaters, can make a superb paste by simply softening with warm water and kneading with a binder such as raw eggs or wheat gluten. John prefers to use both in his pastes.

For several years I caught a good number of carp from my local waters on an extremely simple base mix of one part Casilan (calcium caseinate) to two parts Beemax (wheatgerm) to which colouring and flavouring were added, plus water. My favourite colours were black, brown and green with flavourings of butterscotch, maple or caramel. Certain combinations seemed important at the time, but looking back I think almost any dark, sweet paste would have scored, as long as it was introduced regularly.

Mixing and kneading this and most other milk-derivative pastes is unfortunately always a sticky affair, though invariably justified by the results. Contrary to popular belief, it is possible to freeze these pastes once mixed, but they do need reworking again after defrosting. For the best results, store the paste in the freezer tightly packed into an airtight plastic container such as an ice-cream carton.

Trout-pellet Paste

Please regard this as a very broad heading embracing virtually all fish-food pellets. These range from those that come in expensive-looking tubs at the local garden centre, for feeding exotic species such as koi carp, to the various-sized pellets manufactured for rearing game species such as trout and salmon, and which are available as both floaters and sinkers. You can even include pig pellets, rabbit pellets and chicken pellets, because with a little thought any of these can be made into super pastes simply by mixing with warm water, plus a binder.

If you have access to a grinder or food blender (a mortar and pestle will do) with which the pellets can be reduced to powder, so much the better. It is then a simple matter to add warm water plus a raw egg or two and knead. If not, put a couple of pints of pellets into a shallow tray and sprinkle them liberally with hot water (shake them about) until they are all completely saturated, but not swimming. Leave them for an hour, for all the water to be absorbed and the pellets to soften, and then knead them into a paste. This can prove rather a messy job, especially if you have been too generous with the water. But don't despair, just keep adding cornflour (plain flour will do) until the khaki-coloured paste becomes nicely pliable. If it crumbles and obviously would not stay on the hook (pellets differ enormously in consistency) knead in two or three raw eggs. Alternatively, use wheat gluten or egg albumen as a binding agent.

The only additive I have ever used with trout pellets to good effect (they are, after all, a complete food in themselves) is Phillips' yeast mixture. Simply sprinkle a tablespoonful over the dampened pellets before kneading them, if your stomach can stand the smell. Not advisable with a hangover, I might add. But the pungent aroma certainly has a special 'something' to which carp are instantly attracted.

Pellet-form food sold at aquarium and garden centres invariably floats, since its purpose is to encourage coloured fish up to the surface so that they can be seen. Not surprisingly, floating pellets are an invaluable attractor when catching carp off the top. But if you shop around and specifically ask for sinking pellets, there is nothing more convenient for loose feeding and prebaiting. Sinking pellets are available in sizes from 10 mm down to tiny 2 mm granules, which are marvellous for scattering by the handful or catapulting around your paste hookbait. All pellet-derived pastes can be stored in polythene bags in the freezer for future use.

Meat in tins

That time-honoured tip of always keeping a tin of luncheon meat in your tackle bag or car boot remains as sound as ever. For tench, chub, barbel and, of course, carp, tinned meats are not only readily accepted, often with unbelievable aggression, but are also cheap, easy to use, last almost indefinitely unless opened and are readily available. What more can you ask of a manufactured bait?

Under this heading I put first and foremost good old luncheon meat in its dozens of different brands, followed closely by tinned ham, chopped pork roll, bacon grill and so on, the only exception being corned beef, which is just too crumbly as a hookbait. As a paste, though, kneaded with cornflour and bound together with the help of a raw egg, corned beef might well be a winner. I haven't tried it, but go on, prove me wrong!

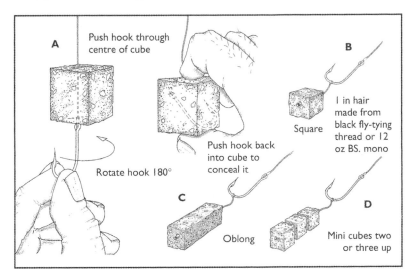

A
Push hook through centre of cube

Rotate hook 180°

Push hook back into cube to conceal it

B
Square
1 in hair made from black fly-tying thread or 12 oz BS. mono

C
Oblong

D
Mini cubes two or three up

Presenting tinned meat (luncheon meat etc.) in cubes or oblongs.

63

Whatever the make, whatever the brand, and regardless of their density, meat cubes always work better for species like chub, barbel and carp if presented in conjunction with a carpet of loose-fed stewed hempseed. Don't stick to large squares only. Dice them into mini cubes, oblongs, and offer on a hair rig for more confident bites. (See diagram on page 63)

For me, the main advantages of tinned meat are that it can be cubed or cut into oblongs (or triangles) with a sharp knife and it remains firm on the hook. Some types and brands are rather fattier, and thus far more buoyant, than others, which makes them extremely useful for presenting over thick bottom weed or debris. Others are more dense, and so stay on the hook longer in strong currents, or are more resistant to the attentions of small nuisance species such as gudgeon, roach or rudd. Experiment with various brands until you find one to suit the particular situation.

As for presentation, the secret of using meat is to be confident that your cube does not fly off the hook on a firm cast. Cut it into cubes of equal size (with a sharp, long-bladed knife) no longer than the shank of the hook being used. This is imperative, as can be seen from the diagram. Gently push the hook downwards through the top of the cube and pull it through at the bottom by gripping the bend with thumbnail and forefinger. Now rotate the hook and ease it into one corner of the cube, pulling gently on the line so that it becomes completely embedded in the meat and hidden from view without the eye of the hook protruding from the top of

Relaxed yet expectant, a barbel enthusiast legers a cube of luncheon meat among the shallow, weedy gravel runs on the Dorset Stour at the famous Throop Fishery near Holdenhurst.

Above: Rigged 'off the hook', on a fine-hair made from black fly-tying thread, with a short, fixed paternoster swan shot leger is, without question, the most effective way of presenting baits such as luncheon meat to wary barbel and chub.

Meat in skins offers even more variety than tinned brands. With a sharp knife it may be cubed, cut into oblongs and hair rigged, or presented straight on the hook in the same way as a cube of luncheon meat. As a change from using hempseed as a bottom attractor, try sinking trout-pellet granules: with meat it is a winning combination.

65

the cube. The hook, will, however, slice neatly through the meat and into the fish on the strike (see diagram).

When barbel or carp in hard-fished waters refuse meat presented on the hook, rig it on to a 1-in fine hair, to give them greater confidence (see diagram). Alternatively, change the shape to an oblong and present it on a hair if it appears that fish have become scared by a square bait (see diagram). Another ruse is to dice the meat into mini cubes and present two or three on a hair (see diagram).

Why it should be, I have never been able to fathom, but cubed meat presented over a carpet of stewed hempseed — whether you are legering or float-fishing the lift method for carp, or quivertipping or stret-pegging for barbel and chub — must be the all-time-best combination of loose feed and hookbait. It does no harm to dice a block of meat up into tiny hempseed-sized cubes for mixing in with the loose feed.

Meat in skins

Everything I have said about the presentation of tinned meat also applies to meat in skins once it is cubed or cut into oblongs. A wonderful choice is available from the local delicatessen or supermarket's chilled meat counter, and tench, barbel, chub, carp and even catfish simply adore it. The trouble is, I also love spicy sausage meats and invariably wolf down far more than the fish I am after.

Among meats in skins I include ordinary pork or beef bangers (cooked and left to cool), chipolatas precooked in tins, tinned cocktail mini sausages, saveloys, garlic-based German sausage, black pudding, Pepperami, salami and the like. The list is as varied as you want it to be, and so there is always a change bait available should carp, for instance, start to wise up to a particular type or brand.

You have the option of dicing the sausage (in some instances it is best to remove the skin, in others, leave it on) into tiny cubes and using a large one either on the hook or presented on a fine hair. Or you can offer it over a bed of attractor particles such as stewed hempseed or red dari seeds (see page 103).

Another attractor I regularly use when presenting meat cubes is extra-fine sinking trout pellets in granular form (see Trout-pellet paste, page 62). A handful scattered into the swim or around the bait every so often works wonders.

Raw meat

When I was a nipper living in Enfield in North London, I regularly fished the local ponds with my grandad, who would always insist on taking along, in addition to our carefully prepared breadpaste and tin of 'gentles', a piece of fresh calf's or pig's liver for bait. I thought he was barmy, of course. But every now and again 'Pops' would whack into a sizeable common carp.

I'm not suggesting that liver and raw steak are anything more than just alternative options worth trying on occasion. But the fact remains, fish are really attracted to the blood, and I have regularly used raw steak successfully as a stand-by when in remote parts of the world, for both fresh and saltwater species. Catfish, especially, quickly home in on liver and raw steak, but it is imperative to change the bait regularly, since the blood dissipates, leaving the meat pale and unattractive.

Cut steak into suitable strips or chunks and hook it as with a lobworm, once only, with all the point and barb of the hook exposed. A cube of liver is best presented on a fine hair rig off the hook. Try raw meat for carp, chub, eels and catfish. You won't be disappointed. For eels and catfish, make up a few balls of groundbait (to deposit around the hookbait) from a mixture of brown breadcrumbs and fresh blood. Your local butcher will oblige.

Cheese

Traditional hard and processed cheeses, as opposed to the soft ones which are spread straight from the tub, make great baits for chub, barbel and carp. It is well worth exploring the cheese counter in your supermarket, because in addition to cheeses such as Cheddar, Red Leicester and Double Gloucester, which don't crumble when cut, there are many smoked and processed cheeses, all of a suitable consistency for cutting, using a really sharp, thin-bladed knife, into ½-in cubes or oblongs for presentation on a fine-hair rig (see diagram).

In waters where small species continually peck away at most baits, go for the rubbery cheeses, which are just as effective as boilies, I can thoroughly recommend Subenhard and Danbo from Denmark, Maasdan, Edam and Gouda from the Netherlands, Swiss Emmental and Gruyère and Jarlsberg from Norway. Also from Norway, the somewhat softer Gjetost is made from goats' milk and has a sweet, caramelized flavour.

For use as loose feed, dice a block into hundreds of mini cubes and scatter these into stillwater swims by hand or with a catapult. For barbel and chub in fast, deep swims, mini cubes can either be deposited by bait dropper, at close range, or at longer range with a large, heavy block-end feeder with the holes enlarged. Give a hefty pull on the feeder as it touches bottom, to ensure instant dispersal of the cubes. A cheese cube presented over a carpet of stewed hempseed is a winner in both still and running water.

67

Pasta

Packet macaroni in $\frac{3}{4}$-in pieces can easily be made into a superb carp bait that chub also will take readily. It is the most useful of the many varieties of pasta as a hookbait.

For every cupful of macaroni you intend to prepare (remember it swells), put one cupful of water into a saucepan. Bring the water to the boil and add a teaspoon each of powder colouring and flavouring for each three cups of macaroni. Simmer for 10 minutes. Finally, drain off all the surplus liquid and allow the beautifully coloured macaroni to cool for half an hour before using or storing in a polythene bag in the freezer.

Macaroni accepts colour readily, and you will be delighted with yet another attractive particle-type carp bait to experiment with. Use a size 6 hook and gently work it through the macaroni tube, bringing the point and barb out $\frac{1}{4}$ in short of the end.

Other manufactured baits

Sinking Dog Treats

Numerous dog treats are displayed on the shelves of your local pet stores, just screaming out to be used as carp baits. Colours and sizes vary and so does the format, from moist lumps to rings. My favourites — I sound like a dog, don't I — are manufactured by Frolic. They are available in various flavours and colours, and come in the form of rings of $\frac{3}{4}$-1 in in diameter, rather like a mini doughnut. Being firm, and rubbery in consistency, they thwart the attention of small fish and are easily threaded singly, or even two up, on to a hair rig. They are perfect for fishing over a bed of hempseed, stewed wheat or maize, where little fish can prove a nuisance. Use a strong hair in conjunction with a size 4 hook.

When baiting with cheese, don't limit yourself (and the fish) to plain Cheddar. In both aroma and texture, there is a wonderful choice from which to choose and experiment.

69

CHAPTER THREE

FLOATERS

··

In addition to breadcrust and casters, just about anything found edible by surface feeders, carp in particular, is worth considering if it floats or can be made to.

Mixers

Sold under the Pedigree Chum label, these are by far the most effective and versatile of all floating carp baits. They work very well in their neutral biscuit colour straight from the box or bag. Buy them in bulk packs, which are much cheaper. Alternatively, try one of the four coloured mixers marketed by Richworth. These are available in blue, orange, yellow and red, and impregnated with extra sweeteners and enhancers.

You can also flavour and colour mixers yourself. I doctor them by frying gently for a few minutes in a rich sauce made from finely grated garlic and butter. No doubt you will come up with your own concoctions.

Being dense, small and square, mixers catapult well and are fairly impervious to the attentions of small fish, though not coots, moorhens, ducks, geese or swans.

To prepare mixers for easy hooking, hold a double handful under the tap until all are wet, and then put them into a polythene bag. Twenty minutes later they will have absorbed the moisture and may be side-hooked (leave the barb and point exposed) or presented singly or two or even three up on a floating hair rig in conjunction with a small floating controller such as the tenpin (see diagram).

To prepare mixers for hookbaits, a friend simply puts a couple of handfuls plus a slice of fresh bread into a polythene bag and leaves them overnight. By the morning they have absorbed all the moisture from the bread and are perfect for hooking.

Once carp wise up to the shape and size of mixers, explore all the many varieties in the local pet stores of biscuit-type cat and dog foods which float.

Cat and Dog Biscuits

There are many widely available cat biscuits, in a range of flavours including pilchard, liver, tuna, duck, rabbit and beef, and in all sorts of shapes and sizes, from ovals to stars. All of them catch carp if prepared and presented like mixers (see

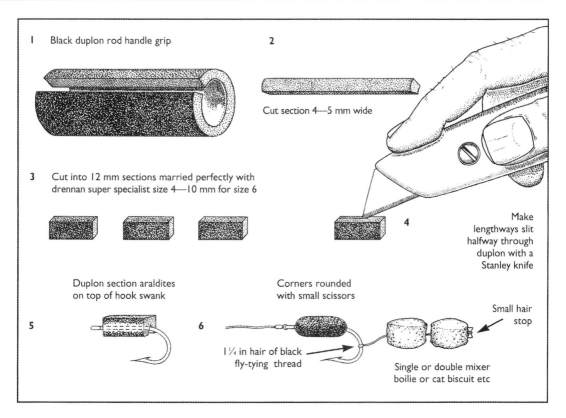

1. Black duplon rod handle grip

2. Cut section 4—5 mm wide

3. Cut into 12 mm sections married perfectly with drennan super specialist size 4—10 mm for size 6

4. Make lengthways slit halfway through duplon with a Stanley knife

Duplon section araldites on top of hook swank

Corners rounded with small scissors

Small hair stop

5.

6. 1 ¼ in hair of black fly-tying thread

Single or double mixer boilie or cat biscuit etc

Hair rigging for presenting floaters.

diagram). Do not limit your choice to those packed in boxes. Many different varieties are sold by weight, and a visit to a specialist pet shop should prove well worth while. Experiment too with dog biscuits.

Boilies

To completely eradicate the nuisance of aggressive surface-feeding species such as rudd, floating boilies are the answer, whether offered side-hooked or presented on a hair (see diagram). You can purchase ready-made shelf-life floaters in a variety of colours and flavours from 10 mm up to 20 mm in diameter, or make commercial or home-made boilies buoyant by putting a batch on a shallow baking tray in a preheated oven for 8–10 minutes. You can also microwave them to achieve the same result. Timing is critical, and one and a half to two minutes should suffice, depending on the base mix of the boilies. (See Making Pop up Boilies, page 87).

Another way of making any sinking boilie float is to use a Marvic boilie punch and pop-up foam kit. The hollow-tube punch removes a core from any boilie of 14 mm or larger, and this is quickly replaced by foam. Once the foam has been fully inserted, simply plug the hole with a section of the core after rolling it between thumb and forefinger to make it more manageable.

71

Above: Mixer-type dog biscuits, in both brand packs and in bulk... cat treats... floating and sinking trout pellets... boilies... marshmallows... sunflower seeds... British carp have never had it so good!

Right: A sight to warm the hearts of all carp fishermen: beneath the shade of an overhanging alder, a dozen or more sizeable double-figure fish mop up small floaters with gay abandon.

Above: Having hooked a big carp on a floater presented close to a sunken tree hugging the opposite bank, Ron Smith wades out carefully to stop it from snagging in the entanglement of dwarf pond lily around his feet.

Left: At his own stillwater fishery in Norfolk, John takes great delight in feeding the stock of carp on floating trout pellets during the close season. But in case anyone gets the idea that the fishing is easy, so far as the carp are concerned, it is all very quickly back to square one once his syndicate members start fishing again on June 16th.

Sunflower Seeds

Although sunflower seeds seem an unlikely floating bait, carp (though not in all fisheries) do mop up both the white and the larger striped grey and white seeds. Because of their high oil content, they float beautifully and can be presented either on a hair or directly on the hook. Either way, they need first to be softened. Put a handful into a cup of boiling water and leave them for 10 minutes. Keep them in a polythene bag to retain the moisture.

Floating Trout Pellets

During the close season, in order to feed them up before they get caught again in June and the entire yearly cycle repeats itself, I regularly feed the stock of carp in my two lakes on floating trout pellets. I would even say that as loose floating food they are the best attractor of all. The trouble is, all small fish from 2-in roach and rudd upwards also love them and very soon nibble them away to nothing once they are softened. But where small fish are not abundant, trout pellets are a great attractor floater to use in conjunction with a small, dark, floating boilie presented on a floating hair rig and controller (see diagram).

You should also try the following: when carp are chomping pellets with gay abandon, make up a smooth paste from some pellets (see Trout-pellet Paste, page 62) and mould this over a sliver of foam or breadcrust on the shank of the hook so that it floats (see diagram). It is absolutely deadly. Alternatively, prepare a batch of pellets so that they are rubbery for hooking (see Mixers, page 70) and carefully thread one on to the shank of a size 12 hook. Then add a small cube of brown breadcrust of the same size, which aids buoyancy and counteracts the weight of the hook (see diagram).

Baking your own floaters

Almost any mix used in the making of pastes (see Pastes, page 55) or boilies (see Making Your Own Boilies, page 77) can be baked in the oven and afterwards cut into cubes which float. So if you like catching carp off the top on floating crust, these home-made 'crusts' make a great follow-on bait once carp wise up to bread. You must ensure, however, that any pelleted base-mix ingredients (such as trout pellets or cat biscuits) are ground into dust (use a mortar and pestle). As a rough guide, you require at least double the amount of eggs that you would normally use in, for instance, your favourite or current boilie mix. If the mixture turns out a little dry, simply add more whisked eggs until it reaches a thick, soupy consistency. This is most important if the final result is to turn out rubbery. Don't be afraid of using a few extra eggs.

Whisk the eggs thoroughly (together with any liquid flavouring) to produce lots of air bubbles, then add them to the dry, well-mixed ingredients (including powder colouring) and whisk gently again before pouring the mix into a well-greased or oiled shallow baking tin to a depth of around ¾ in. Smooth the top over with a fork and then put the mix in the middle of a preheated oven set to gas mark 4 (180°C) for 30 minutes. The 'cake' is then tipped from the tray, allowed to cool, and cut with a very sharp long-bladed knife, into cubes of the desired size.

You might like to try the following recipes. Each of the mixes fits perfectly in a 7 x 11 x 1½- in deep baking tray.

2 oz sodium caseinate
4 oz ground cat biscuits (for instance, Brekkies or Meow Mix)
3 oz maize meal
1 oz wheat gluten
1 teaspoon baking powder
1 level teaspoon powder colouring (your choice, but orange looks good)
12 eggs and 1 teaspoon liquid flavouring (your choice)

2 oz sodium caseinate
4 oz ground trout pellets or salmon fry crumb
3 oz semolina or soya flour
1 oz wheat gluten
1 teaspoon baking powder
1 level teaspoon green powder colouring
12 eggs and 1 teaspoon liquid flavouring (optional)

2 oz sodium caseinate
4 oz Sluis CLO bird food
3 oz maize meal
1 oz wheat gluten
1 teaspoon baking powder
1 level teaspoon yellow powder colouring
12 eggs and 1 teaspoon liquid flavouring

Floating Paste

Combining the lightness of sodium caseinate, for maximum buoyancy, with a fibre ingredient such as wheatgerm or Beemax, plus powder colouring and liquid flavouring, creates an effective, truly 'floating paste' in just a few minutes.

Simply add half a teaspoon of liquid flavouring to 12 oz of water and pour into a mixing bowl. Mix 8 oz of sodium caseinate, 2 oz of wheatgerm, plus a level teaspoon of powder colouring (I prefer green and yellow) thoroughly together and add the mix little by little to the water, blending it firmly with

75

Having a go in the kitchen will not only impress the woman of the house (don't let her get used to the idea!), but give you the opportunity to try baking all kinds of floating cakes using the same ingredients as for boilies.

a wooden spoon. Finally, knead the mix with your hands until it is pliable.

Marshmallows

No, I haven't decided to end this section on a humorous note. Marshmallows really do make great floaters for carp. The sweet ingredients, including glucose, starch, gelatine and syrup, plus flavouring and colouring, would do any modern carp bait justice. Besides, marshmallows float exceptionally well, certainly for up to an hour, whether introduced whole or cut into halves or even quarters.

Make certain the point and barb are exposed for penetration on the strike when hooking them on. Personally, I much prefer mounting them on a hair with the hook completely free (see diagram), with a strip of duplon glued to the hook so that it floats on the surface and does not hang down and inhibit a carp from sucking in the bait.

As marshmallows are quite heavy, when you are fishing at close to medium range a controller is seldom needed unless you have cut them into halves or quarters. In any event, quarter several for freebaiting to allow the carp to acquire a taste for them.

CHAPTER FOUR

MAKING YOUR OWN BOILIES

Almost any combination of the ingredients listed in this chapter, even the most crumbly concoction, if mixed with enough of a binder such as wheat gluten and beaten egg, can be kneaded into a paste, rolled into balls either by hand or with the aid of a bait-maker such as the Rollaball, and boiled until the outside skin hardens. This makes it impervious to the

Making your own boilies can be great fun, and once you know what all the various ingredients are used for, it is nowhere near as difficult as you might imagine.

**Simple boilie
presentations.**

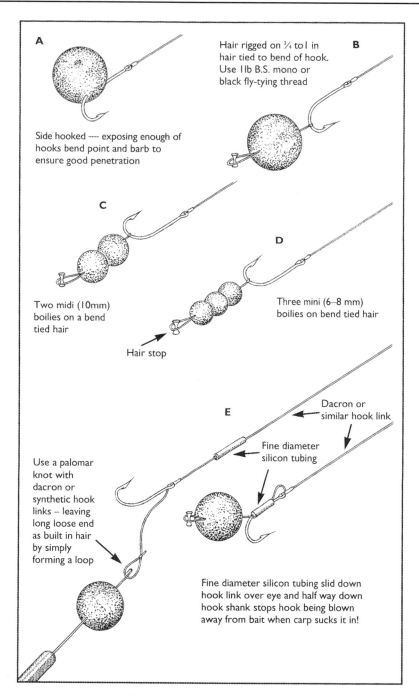

A

Side hooked ---- exposing enough of
hooks bend point and barb to
ensure good penetration

B

Hair rigged on ¾ to1 in
hair tied to bend of hook.
Use 1lb B.S. mono or
black fly-tying thread

C

Two midi (10mm)
boilies on a bend
tied hair

Hair stop

D

Three mini (6–8 mm)
boilies on bend tied hair

E

Dacron or
similar hook link

Fine diameter
silicon tubing

Use a palomar
knot with
dacron or
synthetic hook
links – leaving
long loose end
as built in hair
by simply
forming a loop

Fine diameter silicon tubing slid down
hook link over eye and half way down
hook shank stops hook being blown
away from bait when carp sucks it in!

constant pecking of smaller, nuisance species which could
otherwise fragment and quickly consume the bait before a
carp or a tench happens along.

It is quite possible to get a bait mix totally wrong by
including an excess of sodium caseinate, for instance, which
could fail to harden and so result in a softish, lop-sided bait
when boiled. But then, dare I say, this the essential challenge

of making your own baits. Never despair when things go wrong: at the very worst you have wasted a few ingredients that you were going to throw in the lake anyway. Simply laugh at your own mistakes while learning, and trust to trial and error until you are happy with the results.

Space restricts me from listing the full range of ingredients which can be used to make boilies. Below, however, is a fairly comprehensive list of popular, proven ingredients, all of which are readily available from specialist tackle shops, corn merchants, pet shops and health food stores.

High-protein Milk Derivatives (Group 1)

Casein is the main or major protein contained in cows' milk. It is refined in various ways and provides the standard, accepted base for HNV (high nutritional value) baits. Casein is available in three types:

30-mesh casein is the coarsest powder and ideal if you want boilies of a really hard consistency for use when pecking species prove troublesome.

80-mesh casein is a much finer powder, perfect for softer-centred boilies and for making floaters.

rennet casein is a more refined, mineral-rich, highly nutritious milk protein (part of the dietary requirements of athletes) for making top-quality HNV baits. It is, in fact, the finely ground and sieved powder of the dried curd from fresh pasteurized skimmed milk. Whether fish actually appreciate this level of sophistication is, of course, debatable. And besides, rennet casein is also more expensive.

Sodium caseinate is a light, sticky (when mixed) soluble casein which is ideal for making both boilies and pastes more buoyant. The more you put in the mix, the more buoyant they become. (See Baking Your Own Floaters, page 74).

Calcium caseinate is sold by chemists as Casilan and is far less sticky than sodium caseinate. It can be used as the HNV base instead of 30 x 80-mesh or rennet casein.

Lactalbumen is also a highly nutritious cows' milk derivative that can be mixed with casein or caseinate to from a more balanced HNV base.

Soya isolate is the isolated protein (the richest part) of the soya bean, which, if used in conjunction with any of the above milk proteins, forms an excellent balanced bait.

Animal and Fish Meal Ingredients (Group 2)

Meal and bone meal is a mixture of dried animal flesh, bone, blood and marrow ground into a fine powder. It is a base ingredient full of protein and has an attractive aroma.

White fish meal is a powder produced from dried ground white fish. It can be mixed in as part of any fish or meat base

79

To reduce pellet-form foods, cat or dog biscuits, even coarse bird feed to a fine powder in readiness for mixing, a mortar and pestle are invaluable — unless you can lay your hands on a coffee grinder.

mix or as the main base ingredient by itself.

Shrimp meal is a smelly, coarse meal produced from dried ground shrimps. It can be used either with equal parts of white fish meal, or by itself as a base ingredient.

Trout pellets and salmon fry crumbs are khaki-coloured, strong-smelling pellets manufactured from various fish meals as a complete food for rearing trout and salmon. Carp and tench simply adore them. Ground down into a fine powder (use a mortar and pestle or a coffee grinder), they make a superb base without the need for any additional colour or flavouring – just egg and gluten. (See Trout-pellet Paste, page 62, and Baking Your Own Floaters, page 74.) The red-coloured pond food pellets sold at aquarium centres for feeding koi carp may be used in the same way.

Liver rowder is a rich, nutritious, strong-smelling powder for use in all HNV bases and also in simple base mixes.

Bird-food and Seed Ingredients (Group 3)

Robin Red is a famous food used for conditioning and intensifying the colour of canaries. Manufactured by Haith Seeds from various seeds, meals and special red food colouring, proven base ingredient but stains your hands.

Soft Bill is another Haith Seeds bird food, formulated specifically for mynahs, among other birds. It is based on soya-bean meal and also includes various seeds, so that it makes an attractive base.

Nectarblend is a rearing food for canaries and budgerigars. It is based on biscuit meal to which various seeds, honey and dried egg yolk have been added. This is yet another superb base ingredient from Haith Seeds.

Sluis Mynah, a well-known bird food and conditioner, is a fairly coarse mixture of cereals, milk derivatives, seeds, vitamins, oils, fats, minerals, vegetables, plus meat and animal derivatives. It is best, before bait making, to sieve off with a maggot riddle or similar the large items such as raisins. This is a great boilie and paste base. (See Sluis Bird-food Pastes, page 60.)

Sluis Universal is a much coarser blend of sugars, fruits, cereals, minerals, oils, vitamins and fats. It also contains raisins, so sieve off any large bits before mixing.

Sluis CLO is a fine powder, both food and conditioner, blended specifically for canaries and other cage-birds. This is a superb, easily mixed base for boilies, and rolls well. It is also great in paste and when baking your own floaters. (See Pastes, page 60, and Baking Your Own Floaters, page 74.)

'Bulk' or 'Carrier' Bait Base Ingredients (Group 4)

Soya flour is the finely ground flour of the most important food bean in the world. It can be used in conjunction with any of the caseinates to form an HNV mix, or as a bulk binding agent in any low to medium-protein bait, such as bird foods, shrimp meal or trout-pellet mixes.

Semolina is most commonly used as a bulking ingredient for making inexpensive, simple carrier-type baits. It makes great pastes and can be used in baking floaters. (See Pastes, page 60, and Baking Your Own Floaters, page 74.)

Maize meal is another invaluable, inexpensive bulk ingredient for simple mixes, and is made from ground plate maize. It is also used in groundbaits, pastes, and in baking floaters. (See Pastes, page 60, and Baking Your Own Floaters, page 74.)

Layers mash, a cheap mixture of various ground cereals, is used as chicken feed, and can be effectively used in simple bulk baits, or to bulk out bream or tench groundbaits when mixed with either bran or breadcrumbs.

Molasses meal, the coarse, strong-smelling meal produced by grinding molasses cane, has a high sugar content. To provide bulk and flavour, add 2–3 oz at a time to any low to medium-protein mix.

Peanut meal is an effective ingredient high in oil and protein, of which up to 50 per cent can be used in a mix.

Hazelnut meal is, like peanut meal, full of protein and oil, and is a fine bulk base ingredient.

Wheatgerm, and a slightly more refined product sold by chemists under the brand name Beemax, is a bulk additive mainly used in pastes and floating baits (see Pastes, page 60, and Baking Your Own Floaters, page 74) and in small quantities only, 1–2 oz at a time, in virtually any boilie mix.

81

Binders and Skinners (for all baits) (Group 5)

Egg albumen is the white of eggs in dry powder form and can be used as a replacement for real eggs. Water must be added in order for the final mix to be kneaded. Some 2–3 oz of egg albumen per 16 oz of mix should suffice plus 9–10 oz of water. Egg albumen also helps make baits harder, so 1 oz may be added (if required) to virtually any base mix.

Vitamealo and Lactopro can almost be considered one and the same ingredient — a low protein calves' milk derivative possessing a distinctive 'ice-cream' aroma. It will put a skin on most baits without the addition of eggs. Again, water must be added.

Wheat gluten is the protein remaining from wheat flour once the starch has been removed. It is a fabulous binder for all boiled baits, holding together the crumbliest ingredients, and so is an excellent addition to pastes (such as ground trout pellets) which easily fall apart. (See Pastes, page 60.) An ounce of wheat gluten is also used in the baking of floaters. (See Baking Your Own Floaters, page 74.)

What bait?

At this point a few words are in order about exactly what constitutes an HNV bait and what does not. The term 'high nutritional value' (HNV) was originally used to describe baits formulated only from various combinations of the high-protein milk derivatives listed in Group 1 above. But today it is also applied to base mixes formulated from a combination of both milk derivatives and bird foods, or fish meals and trout pellets, as in Mix 2 below.

Trout pellets, for instance, are in themselves arguably an HNV bait. They have to be in order for trout to pack on the massive weight ratio of flesh to pellets consumed. And, of course, carp as well as trout love them. It is widely accepted that by offering carp a high-protein milk-derivative bait, you will carry on catching for very much longer than on a low-protein bulk or carrier-type bait (Group 4) because a carp, in effect, knows what is nutritionally better for it. This is a fair enough assumption, and if it is correct then it is obviously pointless investing a fortune in expensive milk-protein mixes if you do not intend putting in extensive effort and time on a particular fishery. An attractive medium or even low-protein mix of the bulk or carrier type (as in Mix 4) will certainly do instead.

Ultimately, much of the modern bait phenomenon is down to confidence. And that is exactly what you are buying in ready-made mixes and prepacks: confidence in a bag. However, one good reason for concocting your own baits is that the knowledge you gain will give you that extra degree of confidence in your approach.

Carp bait manufacturers, such as Richworth Products, Rod Hutchinson Baits, Geoff Kemp and Nutrabaits, give excellent recipe lists for making boiled baits using their ingredients. And, of course, after a little effort and experimenting, you will start concocting your own. To get yourself started, you could try the following recipes for making boilies. They are well proven and include one each from Groups 1, 2, 3 and 4. Group 5 simply contains recommended ingredients for binding and adding a skin to any of the baits you make from combinations within Groups 1–4.

Mix 1: High-protein, HNV milk-derivative bait

3 oz 30-mesh casein
3 oz lactalbumen
6 oz liver powder
2 oz soya isolate
2 oz wheat gluten
1 teaspoon powder colouring of your choice
7 eggs (medium)

Mix 2: HNV fish-meal special

2 oz 80-mesh casein or Casilan
8 oz finely ground trout pellets or salmon fry crumbs
4 oz white fish meal
2 oz wheat gluten
1 teaspoon brown powder colouring
5 eggs (medium)
Plus optional flavouring: 1 teaspoon seafood, shrimp, sea scent, etc.

Mix 3: Bird-food special

2 oz 80-mesh casein or Casilan
4 oz Robin Red
4 oz soya flour
4 oz Sluis CLO
1 teaspoon flavouring, if required
Plus 3 oz egg albumen and 9 oz water (no eggs required)
NB: no colouring is necessary, since there is no way of altering the distinct red of Robin Red.

Mix 4: Inexpensive, low-protein bulk or carrier bait

2 oz calcium caseinate or Casilan
6 oz semolina
6 oz maize meal
2 oz wheat gluten
1 teaspoon flavouring of your choice
1 teaspoon colouring of your choice
5 eggs

83

The easiest way to ensure a creamy paste is to add the well-mixed dry ingredients to the beaten eggs, colour and flavouring in a large bowl.

From a well-kneaded ball of paste, roll out sausages on the work surface until they have the diameter of the boilies required. Then cut these into segments and roll them individually or lay them across a Rollaball bait-maker.

If your paste's consistency is just right, large batches of boilies are easy to churn out with the Rollaball bait-maker. A quick backwards and forwards movement with the rollaball top, and, hey presto, the sausages are turned into balls, all ready for boiling.

Boil your baits in small batches for 1—2 minutes for a skin to form and the ingredients to cook. Most boilies float to the top when they are ready but some, particularly fish meal boilies, will take double the time.

Tip the boiled baits straight from the wire basket and boiling water on to an old towel spread out on the work top. And, ideally, leave them overnight to harden fully.

This common carp succumbed to a pair of 14 mm boilies presented on a 1 in long hair in conjunction with a bolt rig and a 2 oz lead.

You will find bait-making very much easier if you keep to measured quantities, so plan your base mix around a 16-oz unit. It is then simple to work our relative quantities if you require bait in bulk. With a 16-oz mix you will require five to seven medium-sized eggs (depending upon the base mix) for mixing into a thick paste, and once rolled, to put a skin on the boilies.

Alternatively, the eggs may be replaced by 3–4 oz of egg albumen or boilie gel. Either one is added to the mix, which, depending again on other ingredients, should require between 6–10 oz of water added and kneaded in.

Mixing

Using a hand whisk (a fork will do at a pinch) beat the eggs in a large bowl, adding any liquid flavouring and powder colouring if required. In a 16-oz mix, a level teaspoon of flavouring and the same measure of powder colouring is usually sufficient. Add the dry (well-mixed) ingredients a little at a time, stirring briskly with a large wooden spoon. Finally, knead the mix with clean hands to a smooth, pliable consistency something like that of soft plasticine, adding an extra egg if the mix appears too dry and crumbly. If eggs are not available, or you have used egg albumen as the skimming agent, add both liquid flavouring and the powder colouring to the water before mixing. Note that too many eggs in certain mixes could well result in the baits floating after boiling. If this occurs, replace the fluid of one or two of the eggs with plain water, or instead of some of the light ingredients (caseinates)

85

use heavier bulk ingredients such as maize meal, semolina or fish meal.

The longer you knead the paste before rolling, the more air you squeeze out, which makes it denser and helps the resulting boilies to sink. Should the mix turn out far too wet and sticky, knead in a little soya flour or semolina until it is nicely pliable. Once the ball of paste is of the desired consistency, break off chunks and roll them out firmly on the kitchen work surface into long sausages with roughly the same diameter as the boilies you require. Then cut them into equal-sized segments with a sharp knife, rolling each between the palms of your hands to form a smooth ball.

Alternatively, invest in one of the Rollaball bait-makers sold by Gardner Tackle, which takes all the hard work out of converting the sausages into balls. Rollaballs are available in both short and long-base models (the latter make more at a time) which form balls from tiny particles of 8 mm in diameter to gobstoppers of 24 mm.

You simply put a line of sausages (of the desired diameter) on the preformed base, work the top backwards and forwards briskly over them a few times, and hey presto, a pile of perfectly shaped balls, all ready for boiling. When you are knocking out large quantities of bait, a large mastic-type bait gun with a range of nozzles, for making different-sized sausages, is a sound, time-saving investment. But you do need to produce a really pliable, non-sticky paste for everything to work smoothly.

If you can't lay your hands on a chip fryer, do not go out and purchase a designer job. For a minimal cost you can buy a wire basket to fit the oldest saucepan in the kitchen (so as not to get on the wrong side of the cook of the house). Three-quarters fill the saucepan with water, bring it to the boil and lower in your hand- (or machine-) rolled baits in the wire basket, around 15–20 at a time. If the amount you lower in takes the water off the boil, you are trying to put a skin on too many at once. I'm afraid there is no short cut here. Much depends on the size of your boilies — whether they are 10 mm minis, 20 mm gobstoppers or standards of around 14 mm. So adjust the amount accordingly.

You generally need to boil the baits for between one and two minutes (a kitchen timer is handy here) for them to be properly cooked and skinned. For tench only, rock-hard baits are not required, so boil for only half the time. The time required can vary dramatically from one mix to another, so start by boiling for a timed minute. Then test by allowing the boilie to cool before plopping it into a glass of water. Fish-meal mixes, for instance, may well need boiling for three or four minutes to make the boilies rock-hard.

Once boiling is complete (remember that the longer they

are boiled, the harder the baits become) gently tip the boilies on to an old towel placed over the work surface and allow them to cool and dry off. After 30 minutes or so, turn them over so that they dry evenly, and in the morning (assuming that you cook in the evening) they can be put in polythene bags and either used immediately or popped into the freezer.

Making 'Pop-up' Boilies

While you are making your own boilies, put to one side a small portion of your ready-kneaded paste, and once all the sinkers have been boiled and left to dry off, roll some paste around mini (8–10 mm) polystyrene balls, known as 'pop-ups'. These are then boiled in the same way and are guaranteed to float, or pop up off the bottom in full view of passing fish.

Alternatively, many brands of shelf-life boilies can be purchased as 'floaters'. Even those which are not, including your own home-made sinkers, can be made to float by extra baking. Simply put a batch on a shallow baking tray and into a preheated oven for 8–10 minutes. Or try microwaving them at a high setting for about a minute and a half, and then testing them in a glass of water once they have cooled off. If they do not float well, cook the next batch for 20 seconds longer, and then test again, repeating the procedure until they do pop up well. But be careful: microwaved boilies have the habit of smoking suddenly.

In some cases baked boilies, for that is what they are, float only for a certain time before becoming waterlogged. If you present them on the surface as floaters, this is a fact of which you quickly become aware. But you will not realize this if the boilie is presented 'popped-up' just above the bottom. In this case the only real solution is to plug the boilie with foam, either during boiling as already mentioned, or with a special tool. The Marvic boilie punch and pop-up kit does this most effectively. Simply remove a core from the boilie with the tube/punch provided (which works with boilies of 14 mm or larger) and replace it with a short section of the dense, pop-up foam. Then plug the hole with a section of the core by rolling it between thumb and forefinger to make it pliable. You can now be absolutely certain that your boilie will pop up to the desired height above the bottom weed, in full view of passing carp.

Ready-made Mixes

If you simply do not want the bother or are unsure about making up your own boilie mix, there are countless pre-formulated balanced mixes available from specialist tackle shops. Indeed there are times, especially during the summer with carp fishing in full swing, when I think my own tackle

87

shop looks more like a grocer's.

Almost every conceivable mix, from milk proteins to bird food, fish meal and seed-based, is now available prepacked with colour enhancers, minerals and vitamins and the rest already added, so you simply add eggs, knead, roll and boil.

Basic mixes such as Richworth's famous 50/50 base, for instance, allow you to add both powder colouring and liquid flavouring, and you also have the option of mixing in an extra ingredient or two. This is really what it is all about. You can, of course, quite happily catch carp on pre-packed frozen or shelf-life boilies from the unbelievable range of colours, flavours and sizes currently available. Or you can get involved in the kitchen and enjoy the extra satisfaction to be gained from catching fish on your very own bait. It's not very different from catching, say, a chub on a natural bait such as a stone loach, brook lamprey or a chunk of wasp-nest cake, having collected these yourself. It all depends on the amount of time you are prepared to spend.

Ready-made Frozen and Shelf-life Boilies

To the best of my knowledge, only one British company has ever offered a range of pre-packed frozen boilies, namely Richworth Baits. These are manufactured by Streamselect, whose freezers are a common sight in most specialist tackle shops around the country. Throughout the 1980s these baits probably accounted for more carp than any other, and were the first pre-packed, ready-to-go boilies available in a choice of sizes, from 8-mm minis up to 14-mm standards.

Shelf-life Prepacks

Richworth now offers the above sizes, plus a 6 mm super mini, a 10 mm midi and larger 18 mm and 24 mm boilies, in their shelf-life range of baits, which come in a huge selection of flavours and colours, as both floaters and sinkers. So do several other well-known manufacturers, including Crafty Catcher, StarmerBaits, Rod Hutchinson and Maestro. The sheer choice of sizes, colours and flavours is mind-blowing. You can go for a sweet or dairy bait, savoury, fish meal, seafood, a seed mix, and so on. Because a packet or two can always be kept in the tackle bag, or a comprehensive selection stored in the car boot even, shelf-life boilies are, along with good old luncheon meat, the most convenient of all manufactured baits.

Most tackle dealers use those they sell and will advise on the density of individual brands, and whether a particular boilie will lie lightly on top of soft silt or weed, or fall through and become hidden. Think also about how the colour will relate to that of the bottom or bottom weed. Will it blend in naturally, or stand out obtrusively? Do you want a flavour that is regularly used on the water you fish, but of which the carp may now have become suspicious? Or is an entirely new smell likely to score, following a few prebaiting stints? These are the questions to ask yourself when selecting a suitable bait. Be choosy.

Opposite: For anglers who haven't the time to make their own, the choice of flavours, colours, sizes and density in pre-packed shelf life and frozen boilies is truly staggering.

CHAPTER FIVE

PARTICLE BAITS

••

The secret of presenting 'particles', which by the handful number in their dozens of even hundreds, as opposed to single baits such as a lump of breadflake or paste, is that bottom-feeding fish become so confident grubbing about and hoovering up numerous small food items (because this is the way they feed naturally) that they are consequently far less suspicious of sucking in the hookbait.

Moreover, once they have been 'drawn' to a particular area by a particle attractor and start feeding aggressively, they will even gulp down much larger offerings without hesitation. For instance, one of the most successful combinations for carp, chub and barbel is a meat cube presented over a bed of stewed hempseed or tares. And surely there isn't a bream or tench living that won't suck up a big, juicy lobworm or a bunch of brandlings once attracted to the swim with either stewed wheat or casters mixed into a cereal-based groundbait. The opportunities for experimenting are immense.

It is worth pointing out that while baits such as casters and maggots are, of course, particle baits, the word 'particles' has over the years become synonymous with grains, peas, beans, nuts and seeds, most of which are cheap, easy to prepare and readily available from many sources. Visit your local pet shop, corn chandler, Indian food shops and health food shops, where you will be amazed at just how many potential fishing baits there are waiting to be tried. Most specialist tackle shops also stock many of the more popular particles in dried form, prepared and ready to use in vacuum packs — even ready-coloured.

The only word of warning I would issue about fishing particles is that you should always ensure they are properly soaked and stewed before use. Not only are they then more manageable for presentation both on and off the hook (as with a hair rig), loose seeds finding their way along the margins will not germinate and sprout, thus introducing alien plants to our indigenous stock of wild flowers. But very much more serious is the accidental damage and possible premature death which could occur in certain species through the expansion of uncooked nuts or grains inside the stomach. Indeed, on some of my local Norfolk tench and carp fisheries, particle baits of any kind, except sweetcorn, have been banned. This is a great pity and a sad reflection of attitudes and the state of coarse fishing in the 1990s.

Over the years all kinds of stories about particles have emanated from waters where fish, and carp in particular, are found dead, their bellies unnaturally bloated. As a fishery owner, I have always listened with great interest. After all, carp of a desirable, catchable size are certainly not cheap to purchase. And yet, having fished with stewed peanuts, for instance, for well over a decade, using them regularly on both my own two stillwater fisheries and local club lakes and pits, I have yet to come across a single carp death caused by them. I have even learnt to recognize certain distinctive individual carp stocked into my own two lakes which are repeatedly caught on peanuts by my syndicate members year after year. Therefore as far as I am concerned — and as I said previously, so long as they are pre-soaked and stewed properly — all particles, including peanuts, are extremely effective baits and no cause for concern.

Sweetcorn

I take my hat off to whoever first tried sweetcorn as a bait and passed the tip on. It is now common knowledge that this hybrid of the maize plant, which is harvested while young and tender, is an instant winner with non-predatory freshwater species all over the world in both running and stillwaters. Even estuarine sea species, such as the grey mullet, readily accept corn.

Sweetcorn is among the top baits for carp, including crucians, tench, barbel, bream, chub and rudd, roach and dace. And while it is most often used in the summer, the majority of anglers thinking of it as an exclusively warm-weather bait, it can sometimes produce excellent results during cold water conditions, for chub in particular.

Even grayling love sweetcorn's bright-yellow colour. Or is it that unique sweet smell and succulent insides? Unfortunately, wherever small perch abound in sizeable shoals, they too will gobble up the yellow kernels fished static on or off the bottom and even on the retrieve.

For tench and bream, sweetcorn is certainly a fine change bait to breadflake, worms or maggots. Present a single kernel on a size 14 hook, two on a size 12, or three or four up on a size 10. In practice, how many you use depends on the size of the individual kernels. If you economize by buying sweetcorn in bulk freezer packs, the kernels are noticeably larger and very much firmer than those in tins. To really fill up a size 8 or

91

A feast of particle baits: first row, left to right: peanuts, tiger nuts, maize; second row: blue peas, hempseed, black beans, soya beans; third row: red dari seeds, maples, buckwheat, malting barley, mung beans, black lentils; fourth row: red sweetcorn, yellow sweetcorn, stewed wheat, black tares, yellow rice, aduki beans.

6 hook when after carp, barbel or chub, for instance, slip three of four kernels on the hook and slide them over the eye and up the line. Then slip another three or four on to the bend and shank before sliding the others down against them. Another way of creating a good mouthful is to rig up several large kernels on a separate hair, tied direct to the bend of the hook. This creates a real mouthful — useful for crafty specimen fish in clear waters which repeatedly refuse corn slipped directly on to the hook.

Sweetcorn is also very effective as a 'cocktail' bait. Try presenting it on the bend of the hook with a liberal pinch of flake along the shank. Or experiment with maggots and corn, redworms or brandlings and corn, or casters and corn. How about corn plus a cube of luncheon meat? Simply sleeve two or three kernels up the line and down again after burying the hook in a meat cube (see Meat in Tins, page 63). The permutations are limited only by your imagination.

Another ruse worth trying once fish wise up to plain yellow sweetcorn, is to change its colour. This is easily done by dissolving a teaspoon of powder dye (as used for colouring carp baits) into a cupful of hot water and pouring it over the sweetcorn (strain off the juices if it is tinned) placed into a clean bait box. Stir the mix gently until all the kernels are evenly coloured, and then drain the excess fluid off. Red, purple, orange and brown are worth trying. At the same time, incidentally, flavouring may be added. Or, to give yellow sweetcorn a different flavour, strain off any liquid and pop it

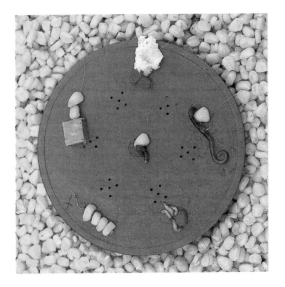 

into a clean polythene bag, adding a tablespoon of, say, oil of anis (the choice is yours) and shake vigorously. After a couple of hours most of the flavour will have been absorbed and the bait is ready to be used straight from the bag, or popped into the freezer.

Stewed Wheat

After returning a catch of tench or bream caught during the summer, you may notice lying in the bottom of the keepnet a residue of regurgitated natural foods in addition to your own hookbait and groundbait fragments. If you look carefully you will notice the seeds of natural grasses, blown into the water by the wind. My point is that many summer species are already tuned into feeding on the swollen grains of grasses as part of their natural daily diet, in addition to eating aquatic insect larvae and crustaceans. This is why stewed wheat is one of the most natural, but underrated and indeed most underused of all particle baits. I urge you to give it a try, whether for prebaiting a new location for carp, or as a bulk groundbait for bream, because wheat is amazingly cheap. You can buy from a farmer or corn chandler a 50-kg (hundredweight) sack of wheat for little more than the cost of a bag of shelf-life boilies or three pints of maggots.

Many of the ponds and estate lakes I fish in Norfolk for tench, carp and bream are most conveniently prebaited with regular sackfuls of wheat, as it is spread along the margins by farmers and wildfowlers to attract mallard and teal in readiness for the shooting season. The benefits to the angler of this common countryside practice are worth bearing in mind.

Wheat is an exceptionally clean bait, easy to prepare and easy to use, and works in both still and running water throughout the summer and autumn. To prepare just enough

Above left: Plain yellow sweetcorn is a great particle bait, but so is red sweetcorn. Or how about trying sweetcorn cocktails, adding worms, breadflake, meat cubes or maggots? When fish are extra shy and spooky you can also hair rig corn most effectively.

Above right: A cupful of wheat put into a vacuum flask with boiling water and left overnight, will provide you with more than enough hookbaits for the following morning.

93

for a day's roach, rudd or dace fishing (chub love it too) on the evening before, pop a cupful of wheat into a large vacuum flask and top it up with boiling water, leaving space at the top for expansion of the grains. In the morning simply pour the wheat into a bait box. Incidentally, wheat swells to three times its size when stewed — a phenomenon my long-suffering mother regularly experienced, with exploding vacuum flasks and blackened saucepans full of wheat and hemp left on the cooker by her irresponsible, fishing-mad teenage son, long after all the water had boiled away. How I never set fire to the kitchen, I don't know.

To prepare large batches of wheat — it is a most effective tench, bream and carp particle — use three times the volume of water to wheat and bring it to the boil in an old saucepan (remember to open the kitchen windows) and leave it simmering for 10 minutes before turning off the heat. Leave it to stew overnight with the lid on.

Alternatively, leave a batch of wheat to soak in cold water for two days, then put it into a plastic bucket with a pull-off lid and cover with boiling water (twice as much by volume).

If you fancy having some fun by colouring wheat, this is the time to add a tablespoon of powder dye and stir in. Red and yellow provide the greatest contrast to its natural buff colour, but the choice is all yours. Press the lid firmly on and leave it, preferably for 48 hours, after which the excess water should be strained off. The grains may not have swelled quite to the size achieved by boiling and simmering or the 'flask' method, but for prebaiting or mixing with a cereal-based groundbait for bream or tench, they will be fine.

Freshly stewed wheat has a wonderful, highly distinctive nutty aroma, and a triangle-shaped split reveals the soft white (flour) inside. For the best results use it immediately. The aroma, I am certain, is part of this bait's very special magic. Alternatively, as with all particles, after preparation stewed wheat may be divided up and stored in polythene bags in the freezer for future use.

Using stewed wheat rather than, say, maggots or casters for roach or rudd, automatically (because of its size) sorts out a better stamp of fish. In fact, my first-ever roach over 2 lb, way back in 1957, caught by trotting a deep weirpool on the River Waveney in Suffolk, accepted stewed wheat.

Bites on wheat are invariably much slower too. But be careful not to overfeed the shoal. Wheat is a heavy, very filling bait. As with sweetcorn, one grain fits nicely on to a size 14 hook, three on a size 10, and so on. Alternatively, for finicky carp or barbel, string several grains on a fine-hair rig off the hook (see diagram).

Maize

Yellowy-orange with a lovely popcorn smell (popcorn is

Presenting particles.

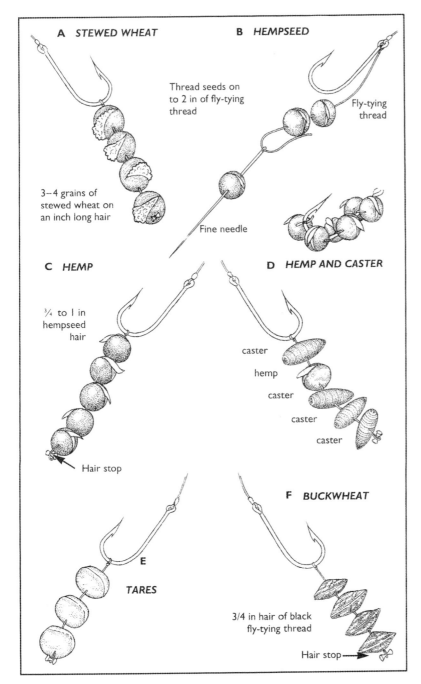

A STEWED WHEAT

B HEMPSEED

Thread seeds on
to 2 in of fly-tying
thread

Fly-tying
thread

3–4 grains of
stewed wheat on
an inch long hair

Fine needle

C HEMP

D HEMP AND CASTER

¾ to 1 in
hempseed
hair

caster

hemp

caster

caster

caster

Hair stop

F BUCKWHEAT

E

TARES

3/4 in hair of black
fly-tying thread

Hair stop

simply exploded maize) and swelling to twice the size of even
a large kernel of sweetcorn, properly prepared maize is a
superb carp bait, totally impervious to the attentions of small
nuisance species.

The only drawback is that preparation does take time,
although in my opinion it is well worth the effort. Start by
soaking the maize for a few days. It will still be rock-hard

95

Although considered by many as just a trotting bait for roach and dace, stewed wheat can be legered most effectively. It is also a great change bait in waters where roach are continually bombarded with maggots and casters.

afterwards, but marginally more receptive to subsequent pressure cooking for a good 20 minutes. Pressure cooking is imperative. Simply boiling it and leaving it to simmer is usually not enough to expand this extremely resilient grain, although I have noticed really fresh maize swells much quicker than old stock, with which you stand no chance. I have left old maize in a tub of water for several weeks, until it stinks to high heaven, yet even in this putrid state it still refuses to swell. Mind you, in the USA, stinking, hard maize is a favourite bait among carp addicts. But not, I hasten to add, with this fisherman.

Once prepared, maize can be put in the freezer in polythene bags until needed. A single grain of maize is none too large for a size 8 hook, which makes it an ideal bait for tench, chub and barbel in addition to carp, whether float-fished or legered. Maize works effectively on a hair rig to overcome the problem of hook-shy fish and, unlike sweetcorn, will stay on when cast long distances.

Pearl Barley

Used in stews and country soups, pearl barley is also a useful fisherman's particle, not only as a binder for making fast-sinking groundbaits (see Groundbaits, page 51) but also as a hookbait and particle attractor. Off-white and smaller than wheat, barley is prepared in exactly the same way. It can also be coloured and/or flavoured during the expansion period, which culminates in a swollen, oval grain around the size of an AAA shot.

During the first half of the century pearl barley was a favourite trotting bait for roach and dace in southern England on rivers such as the Thames. And while today's favourites, such as casters, reign supreme, since shoal fish eventually wise up to the more commonly used offerings, there is good reason for turning the clock back and giving pearl barley a try.

Pearl barley is best presented singly on a size 16 or 14 hook while introducing a dozen or so loose grains every other trot down. Used as a stillwater attractor feed, it is excellent for most cyprinids, particularly tench, bream and carp.

Malting Barley

Being similar in size and colour to wheat, malting barley is best prepared in exactly the same way. When properly stewed, it swells to twice its dried form, splitting lengthways to reveal an off-white inside. It may be coloured with the addition of a teaspoon of powder dye during stewing (yellow, orange and red look terrific) and even flavoured. Present two grains on a size 14 hook, four or five on a size 8, or string half a dozen on to a fine hair tied to the bend of the hook. Like carp and tench, bream too hoover up malting barley, so it can be used like wheat as a bulk additive to cereal-based groundbaits. Even so, in my opinion it is a poor second to wheat.

Rice

Much underrated and rarely used by the vast majority of fishermen, boiled rice is in fact a great bulk additive for making tench and bream groundbaits (see Groundbaits, page 51) and an inexpensive mass-particle attractor for carp. It is virtually impossible to present on the hook, however.

Rice is easy to colour. My preference is for a deep golden-yellow, simply achieved by adding a teaspoon of turmeric to the water when boiling. The powder dyes used for making carp baits also work well. Because rice expands, always add treble the volume of water and leave it to simmer for 15 minutes after it starts to boil. Finally, tip the contents into a colander and leave for a while to drain away the excess water.

Hempseed

Were I limited to the use of just one particle for all my

freshwater fishing, not as hookbait but as a loose-feed attractor, then without hesitation I would choose hempseed, which I truly believe has almost magical qualities. Some say that because of its mussel-like shape and because the stewed seeds sprout tiny white shoots, hempseed is mistaken by fish for tiny pea shell cockles, on which they feed naturally. Others put more importance on its unique aroma and oil content, which permeate the water once it is lying on the bottom. Either way, its pulling powers are without equal, for no other particle attractor puts barbel and carp into a feeding frenzy as quickly as stewed hempseed. In addition, it has the benefit that small nuisance fish tend to leave it alone, which is a godsend when you are fishing in a gin-clear summer river for chub and barbel. Also, while casters and maggots, if not attacked by minnows, bleak or dace, instantly get washed downstream and out of the swim, hempseed settles attractively on the bottom among the sand and gravel, remaining there until barbel or chub find it.

Because hempseed proved so effective in barbel rivers, anglers started gross overfeeding, which led to this fine bait being banned on fisheries such as Throop on the Dorset Stour and the Hampshire Avon's famous Royalty, which is a great pity. There is no need to overfeed: simply attract the fish — two pints is quite sufficient for a day's sport on all but the largest of rivers — and then use a different bait on the hook.

Although hempseed works best purely as an attractor for barbel, carp and chub in conjunction with a cube of meat, casters, maggots, peanuts, corn, tares, maple peas or tiger nuts on the hook, there are occasions when it is worth trying as a hookbait. This can be achieved in two ways (see diagrams). Either wind a string of seeds around a long shank hook, or simply hang a short hair of seeds from the bend of the hook. Other small particles such as casters, tares, buckwheat or maggots can be threaded on along with the seeds (see diagram), but because these rigs take time to arrange, it is not necessary when bites are fast and furious. Keep it as a trick up your sleeve for when fishing is hard.

When you are using hempseed for smaller species, dace and roach in particular, beware of overfeeding, which encourages super-fast bites that are almost impossible to hit. In clear water during the summer, dace and roach can actually be seen 'flashing' as they rise close to the surface, competing for the loose seeds thrown in, and this results in many false bites as they peck mistakenly at the split shot. To overcome this problem wind a length of lead wire around the line a foot from the hook and secure it by bending it over at each end. Fix all additional shots around the base of the float.

For roach and dace, a size 16 or 14 hook is perfect for presenting a single seed. Simply press the bend of the hook into the split. What also invariably improves results is to loose-feed with hemp, just a half dozen seeds every other trot down, while presenting an elderberry, tare or caster on the hook. In cold water conditions a single caster or bronze maggot trotted close to the bottom over loose-fed hemp is a deadly combination for roach and chub.

Preparing Hempseed

To prepare a batch of hempseed (and most other particles) is simplicity itself. You can boil and simmer it in an old saucepan (with the emphasis on 'old') on the cooker for 30 minutes — and completely stink the kitchen out. But far easier is to leave the seeds in cold water to soak for two to three days, then drain the water off, put them into a bucket with a pull-off lid and cover them with boiling water to a depth of 2 in. Press the lid down firmly, and simply leave them to stew and swell in their own juices for a minimum of 24 hours, during which time they will split and darken, almost to black. If you can wait 48 hours, so much the better. For carp fishing I prefer to leave hemp in the bucket for several days, almost until it starts fermenting, when I am sure it has even greater pulling power.

Once the seeds are ready, the surplus water can be strained off and the bait used immediately. Or it can be popped into the freezer, a pint or two to a polythene bag, until required. As it is a bait I use regularly throughout the season for carp, barbel, roach, dace and chub, I prefer to prepare hempseed a gallon or two at a time, as I do with several other particles. This way, it is less time-consuming and very much cheaper.

Tares

As either loose feed or hookbaits or both, tares are preferable to hempseed for some anglers. The preparation of tares is exactly the same as for hemp, and I like to leave tares in the bucket for 48 hours before straining the excess water off and bagging them up for the freezer or immediate use.

Naturally dark brown, tares often work more effectively for trotting if coloured black. Simply add a tablespoon of powder dye (the carp bait kind) in with the boiling water and stir gently to mix well in. To allow for expansion (with one gallon of tares) ensure the boiling water covers them by at least 3 in. For legering and loose-feeding tares for chub, barbel or carp, fix tares three or four up on a short hair (see diagram). Alternatively, simply rely on the tares as loose feed, using a change bait on the hook such as a mini boilie, cube of meat or tiger nuts. For trotting for roach, dace and chub, a single tare fits nicely on a size 14 hook. A winning combination is to feed with tares while using a caster or an elderberry on the hook. Experimenting with hookbait alternatives invariably produces results.

99

Another fine River Wensum barbel safely in the net. It succumbed to a bunch of maggots, having been enticed out from beneath an overhang of willow branches into a clear, gravel-bottomed run by a carpet of loosefed hempseed.

Buckwheat

In its curious angled and dried form, this unusual particle from the Middle East looks incredibly like the shell of a minute Brazil nut and would seem to be anything but a fishing bait. However, being small and dark, it is yet another 'change' particle that can be effectively used for carp, chub or barbel that have been bombarded with all the more popular offerings. Preparation is the same as for wheat, and while two or three grains fit neatly on a size 8 hook, once softened and split, buckwheat is also very effectively presented on the hair rig, whether legered or float-fished (see diagram). Try a single grain on a size 14 hook when loose-feeding hempseed or tares for roach, dace and chub.

Tick Beans

Prepared in exactly the same way as wheat, this large, shiny, dark-brown bean is deadly for carp as both loose feed and hookbait, or simply as a hookbait presented over a bed of hemp, tares, buckwheat or maple peas. It is certainly among the top six particle baits for carp.

Tick beans can be legered and/or float-fished beneath a 'lift rig', either side-hooked or offered two up on a hair. They are a most reliable bait for casting long distances, totally impervious to the attentions of small nuisance species which rip softies and wheat to bits in minutes. Try them for barbel when loose-feeding with tares or hempseed.

Maple Peas

I once reared a squab (fledgling pigeon) by having to chew into pulp and then regurgitate twice a day an entire mouthful of softened maple peas. They are certainly not my idea of food, but like most small, dark particles, maple peas are adored by carp. Preparation is exactly the same as for wheat, and the results may be frozen if not used immediately.

Once softened, maples may be side-hooked two up on a size 8 hook or threaded on to a hair with a baiting needle, three or even four up. Use both as loose feed and hookbait, or as a change hookbait only, presented over a bed of tares or hempseed. They are well worth trying for barbel and chub.

Blue Peas

Years ago blue peas (a pale greenish-blue version of maples) were soaked and mixed into soups and stews. Perhaps they still are, but it is mostly pigeon fanciers who buy them nowadays — and carp fishermen. Preparation and presentation

Without question, well stewed peanuts are a fabulous carp bait, whether legered or float-fished 'lift style', the method John employed to lure this lean double-figure fish.

101

are exactly the same as for maples, though blue peas are generally much less effective, probably because of their lighter colour.

Peanuts

I have to admit that I am a peanut addict. I also rate them very highly indeed as a carp bait, or simply as a hookbait presented over a bed of much smaller particles such as hemp, buckwheat, maples, tares or red dari seeds. Better still, in my opinion, is to loose feed with standard-sized nuts and on the hook offer giant American peanuts. These, once swollen, may be side-hooked singly on a size 6 hook or two up on a size 4, but ensure that the point and barb are exposed for clean hooking. Alternatively, whether legering with a bolt rig or presenting peanuts beneath a simple lift rig — my favourite method with this bait — sleeve two nuts on to a 1 in hair.

Their tremendous buoyancy makes peanuts ideal for presenting over a weedy or snaggy bottom (see diagram). Where soft weeds prove troublesome, however, use a similar length piece of round, buoyant foam on the hair with the two nuts so that they float well within the carp's vision above the bottom crud. This ruse works with most particles.

In still waters that are extensively baited with peanuts for carp, tench quickly learn to get in on the act and acquire a liking for them. And so do the quality roach. Moreover, if you are attracting barbel or chub into a particular swim by prebaiting with loose-fed hempseed or tares, give peanut hookbaits a try. Simply dice up a few nuts and mix them in with the loose feed so that the fish get used to the taste.

Ready-shelled (unroasted) standard-sized peanuts are perfect for loose-feeding and prebaiting and can be bought from corn

Presenting peanuts

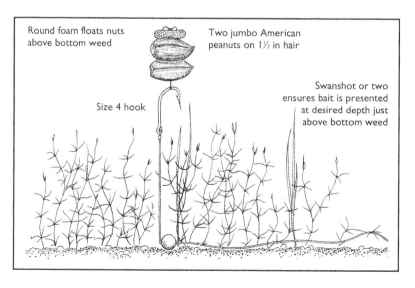

Round foam floats nuts above bottom weed

Two jumbo American peanuts on 1½ in hair

Size 4 hook

Swanshot or two ensures bait is presented at desired depth just above bottom weed

merchants, pet shops and even specialist tackle shops by the pint or in 25-kg (half-hundredweight) sacks. The jumbo American peanuts are available from health food shops and specialist tackle shops.

The method of preparation which swells the peanuts to at least half as big again and makes them rubbery for easy hooking without the two halves coming apart. Like hempseed, nuts are best prepared in bulk in a large plastic bucket with a pull-off lid. To allow for expansion, cover them with boiling water to a depth of several inches and leave them for 48 hours after pressing the lid down firmly. They will be nicely swollen and ready for immediate use or for bagging up and storing in the freezer once any excess water has been strained off.

Tiger Nuts

For carp, I rate these crunchy vegetarian treats as having almost the same pulling power as peanuts. Tiger nuts can be bought from health food shops or specialist tackle shops in bulk or in pint packs already prepared. Care must be taken with their preparation, which is similar to that of maize. Soaking them for a full 48 hours in a bucket of cold water and then pressure cooking them for 20 minutes really softens them up. Alternatively, after the initial soaking, put half a pint at a time (barely covered with water) into a cereal bowl and microwave them on the high setting for 15 minutes.

I love to float-fish tigers on a lift rig along the margins, having loose-fed with them or hempseed. I side-hook the nuts, or where cautious carp are a problem, present them on a hair rig. One nut fits nicely on a size 8 hook, two on a 6 or a size 4. Tiger nuts vary considerably in size and shape, and I have a habit of sorting through and selecting the long ones for hookbaits. They are a great long-distance legering bait as they rarely fly off on the cast.

Sometimes it takes carp several sessions of prebaiting to switch on to this curious-looking new food source. But when they acquire a liking for tiger nuts, action is assured. They also make a good change hookbait for barbel and chub in conjunction with loose-fed buckwheat, tares or hempseed.

Red Dari Seeds

These interesting little seeds, which come from the Middle East, once prepared (as for wheat) make an exceptionally fine particle attractor for carp. Like wheat, they benefit from being left to slightly ferment in their own juices for a few days. Colour alone sets them apart from other mass particles in that they are of mixed colours, from buff to dark brown, and so a carpet of daris is not instantly frightening to an approaching carp. As they are small, the seeds are best presented several at

103

Right: Simple shock rig for particles and boilies.

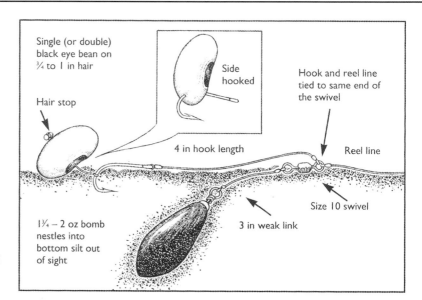

Single (or double) black eye bean on ¾ to 1 in hair

Side hooked

Hook and reel line tied to same end of the swivel

Hair stop

4 in hook length

Reel line

Below: Float-fishing particles such as tiger nuts at close quarters demands the utmost stealth and concentration. John prefers to kneel so that he is close to the water, holding the rod throughout for an instant strike.

1¾ – 2 oz bomb nestles into bottom silt out of sight

3 in weak link

Size 10 swivel

a time on a fine-hair rig and a size 8 or 6 hook. This is an effective bait when fished over a bed of tares or hemp, or used as both loose feed and hookbait.

Mung Beans

Small and pale green, mung beans are prepared exactly the same way as wheat. As with most particles, if you have the time, soaking them beforehand in cold water for 48 hours will produce maximum expansion during stewing. Present three or

104

Colouring white particles such as black-eyed beans could not be easier. All you need is a bucket with a rip-off lid, a spoonful of powder dye, a spoonful of flavouring, and boiling water.

It is sensible and very much cheaper to colour and flavour particles in bulk. Then pack them into polythene bags and store them in the freezer for future use.

four beans on a fine hair and a size 8 hook, whether float fishing or legering in conjunction with a bolt rig.

Mung beans are not in the same league as hempseed as an attractor, but carp do respond to them in well-stocked waters, whether used purely as a hookbait over a bed of hemp or as both loose feed and hookbait.

Black-eyed Beans

These beans, widely available from health food stores, can also be bought in specialist tackle shops, which sell them by the sack, by the pint, and even ready-prepared. Black-eyes can also be purchased in tins, but it is far better and considerably cheaper to buy them in dried form in bulk and prepare them yourself.

This off-white salad bean with a distinctive black 'eye' can easily be stewed, coloured and flavoured to suit any purpose. It is therefore one of the most versatile of all particles for carp, which, in the vast majority of fisheries, respond quickly to prebaiting with it.

Preparation is the same as for peanuts, with the addition of a tablespoon each of powder colouring and flavouring. Be sure to cover the beans with at least half their own volume of boiling water, because their expansion is massive. The permutations of colours and flavours are endless and very

105

much part of the fun gained from preparing these and other particle baits. Colours I have used to good effect are orange, yellow, brown and red, while successful flavours are aniseed, maple, caramel and butterscotch. Experiment for yourself. Why not, for instance, dye the beans jet-black and get them to reek to high heaven with squid extract?

One bean fits nicely when side-hooked on a size 8 and two work well on a size 6 or 4. Make sure that the point and barb go right through and are fully exposed, or penetration on the strike could be impaired. Black-eyes also thread nicely on to a fine-hair rig with the aid of a baiting needle, and, like most particles, work well in conjunction with a simple bolt rig (see diagram).

In waters where black-eyes are extensively used for carp, other species, tench in particular, soon learn to appreciate them, and it is not uncommon to account for the occasional quality roach or rudd, especially when presenting these beans on a lift rig.

Black Beans

I suspect that anyone who enjoys Chinese food will be acquainted with the flavour of this shiny black bean, which is about the same size as a black-eye, and can be prepared, presented, and even flavoured in exactly the same manner. Strangely, though, I have not experienced the same kind of success with this particular bean as I have with black-eyes.

Soya Beans

These creamy-white beans, an important food source all over the world, are halfway in shape between round and oval, and the size of a swan shot. They swell considerably if prepared in the same way as wheat, turning pale yellow. If this colour is not to your liking, simply add a spoonful of powder dye to the boiling water plus the flavouring of your choice.

Soya beans can be side-hooked for float fishing and legering at reasonably close range, one up on a size 8 or two on a size 6. But for distances beyond 25 yards, because of their softness they are best threaded on to a hair rig, say three up on a size 6 hook. They are a very effective particle for carp, and tench also accept them readily.

Chick Peas

These round, creamy-coloured peas are a firm salad favourite throughout Europe and are gaining in popularity in Britain as people turn towards healthier food. Chick peas are available ready-prepared in cans in most supermarkets, but this is a very expensive way to buy them. It is far better to buy them in bulk from health food stores and prepare them yourself, using the same method as for wheat. Chick peas accept colours and flavours readily, which makes them an extremely versatile particle that carp soon latch on to after a little prebaiting.

Since chick peas are almost round, once coloured — deep red is my choice — they look very similar to medium-sized boilies and are presented in the same way. They can be either side-hooked or threaded on a fine-hair rig, with hooks in sizes 8 and 6.

Haricot Beans

In their familiar form as baked beans, haricots are an instant particle in a can, effective both for carp and tench. Although somewhat soft to present, baked beans may be carefully side-hooked for close range float fishing, but are best hair-rigged for legering and presented up to medium range only. Hooks in size 10 and 8 complement this bait nicely. Plain haricot beans are also available in tins, but frankly they are not worth the bother.

Borlotti Beans

These beans are another convenient carp bait available ready-cooked and in a rich sauce in a tin. I find borlottis far superior to baked beans and, since they are slightly larger and firmer, easier to present. Side-hook them for float fishing or thread them on a hair for legering. They work especially well in heavily coloured water as both loose feed and hookbait, or as hookbait only when presented in conjunction with a mass-particle attractor such as hempseed.

Red Kidney Beans

One of the biggest beans available, red kidney beans do not require colouring, but, in their dried form, must be prepared in exactly the same manner as wheat. They are available in bulk packs from health food shops and from supermarkets precooked in cans ready to be mixed with a salad or chilli con carne. Incidentally, unless these particular beans have been thoroughly stewed, it is dangerous to eat them. Red kidneys are a fine carp bait when presented over a carpet of maples, tick beans or hemp, and when used as both hookbait and loose feed. Side-hook them on a size 6 or use two on a fine-hair rig tied to a size 4.

Butter Beans

By far the largest bean, and flat in cross-section, butter beans seem almost designed for fishing over-dense weed or thick silt, where small particles soon disappear. On some waters they produce carp, on others nothing at all.

Butter beans can be bought precooked in tins or in bulk from health food stores. Stew them in the same way as hempseed, adding powder colouring and flavouring if you

107

prefer. Being large, butter beans permit the use of large hooks, and though soft, are heavy enough to be freelined into lily pads on weightless tackle, just like a lump of paste, if you cast with care. They are a good particle for hair-rigging and offering with a 'lift rig'.

Elderberries

Though elderberries are not generally considered a particle bait, I have included them in this chapter because when trotted in conjunction with loose-fed tares and especially stewed hempseed, they are a cracking bait for dace, roach and chub, and I have even caught barbel on them.

The secret is to harvest the berries in the autumn before they become overripe, and bottle them for use at any time throughout the season. If you try to pull them from the stalks they will spoil, so simply cut off little bunches containing 20 or 30 berries and let them drop straight into a preserving jar containing a solution of dilute formalin or glycerine. When required, simply give the berries a good rinse in cold water and present them on a size 16 or 14 hook.

The finest spots for trotting with elderberries are where elder trees hang out over the river and provide the occupants with an autumnal windfall of these juicy purple-black fruits.

Aduki Beans

These mahogany-coloured beans possess a strong but pleasantly nutty aroma, and once prepared, reach double the size of a swan shot, though oval and typically bean-shaped. Simply bring them to the boil in twice their volume of water, to allow for expansion, and simmer for 30 minutes. Then rinse them in cold water or leave to cool. Store them in the freezer in a polythene bag if they are not for immediate use.

An effective particle for carp, aduki beans can be side-hooked singly on a size 10 or three to a 6, or hair-rigged three or four up, and presented over a bed of hempseed or as both loose-fed attractor and hookbait.

Black Lentils

Also called urid whole or black matpe, black lentils, which because of their protruding white shoot look rather like stewed hempseed even before preparation, are readily available from Indian food shops. Some of my carp-fishing friends even rate them on a par with stewed hempseed both as attractor and hookbait, although in my opinion their aroma is not as penetrating. Nevertheless, black lentils, which turn a khaki colour when stewed, are well worth trying in fisheries where the carp are suspicious of all the more commonly used small attractor particles, purely as an attractor or as both attractor and hookbait.

Black lentils can be side-hooked singly on a size 10, two up on a size 8 or 5 up on a hair. To prepare them, bring to the boil in twice their volume of water and simmer for just 10 minutes — any longer and they go mushy. They may then be used straight away or frozen for future sessions. Like hempseed, black lentils prove more effective if left in the water in which they were stewed for a few days before use.

Below: Used in conjunction with loosefed hempseed, long trotting elderberries is a superb technique for taking dace, roach and chub throughout the autumn and winter months.

Left: Mounted using a fine baiting needle and a Gardner V hairstop, here are a selection of particles some hair-rigged and others side-hooked, ready for action. First row, left to right: peanuts, blue peas, aduki beans; second row: soya beans, black beans, maize; third row: tiger nuts, maples, black tares.

109

CHAPTER SIX

LIVEBAITS AND DEADBAITS

There are two main considerations when choosing suitable livebaits for catching predatory fish: the availability of bait fish and whether your actions could affect the sport of others. The two go hand in hand really, because wherever a prolific stock of small shoal fish exists, then taking a few for use as bait is not going to stop other anglers enjoying catching them. And this is the moral yardstick by which I suggest taking small fish for livebaits should be considered.

Dace, Gudgeon and Bleak

As I have already mentioned the really tiny species such as stone loach, bullheads and minnows (see Natural Baits, pages 39-42) let us start with dace, gudgeon and bleak. All three make great chub, perch, zander and pike baits. Eels and catfish love them too.

For eels, perch and zander I rate the hyperactive gudgeon as infinitely better than bleak or dace. For perch, hook the fish

Hooking on dace or similar freshwater deadbaits for catfish.

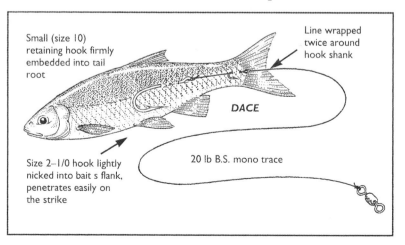

Small (size 10) retaining hook firmly embedded into tail root

Line wrapped twice around hook shank

DACE

Size 2–1/0 hook lightly nicked into bait s flank, penetrates easily on the strike

20 lb B.S. mono trace

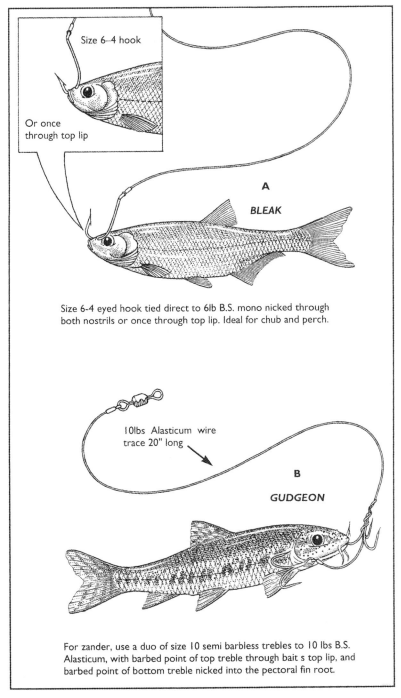

Hooking on small livebaits like dace, gudgeon or bleak.

Size 6–4 hook

Or once through top lip

A

BLEAK

Size 6-4 eyed hook tied direct to 6lb B.S. mono nicked through both nostrils or once through top lip. Ideal for chub and perch.

10lbs Alasticum wire trace 20" long

B

GUDGEON

For zander, use a duo of size 10 semi barbless trebles to 10 lbs B.S. Alasticum, with barbed point of top treble through bait s top lip, and barbed point of bottom treble nicked into the pectoral fin root.

as shown in the diagram. For zander, mount the gudgeon on a duo of size 10 trebles tied to a 10lb Alasticum trace (see diagram) with the top hook through the top lip and the lower one nicked into the pectoral root.

For chub, the silvery bleak is by far the most desirable livebait. The sight of chub repeatedly smashing into bleak

111

Opposite: These pike enthusiasts enjoy hectic sport on Norfolk's Rockland Broad, fully aware that livebaits produce lots of action because they are a vital part of the pike's daily diet.

shoals at the surface is a regular sight throughout the summer and autumn in larger rivers which contain both species, such as the Thames and the Great Ouse system. Use a size 4 hook tied direct and hook the bait fish once only through the top lip or through both nostrils (see diagram).

As a pike livebait (or a catfish deadbait), dace of 5–7in probably outfish everything else. As dace are slim, pike have no trouble in turning them, and provided they are mounted on a sensitive float rig, they will work attractively. Hook pike baits on a duo of size 8 semi-barbless trebles tied to a 15-lb wire trace with the barbed point of the top hook through the top lip and the bottom treble gently nicked into the pectoral fin root (see diagram).

To hook dace and similar species for catfish, use a 20-lb monofilament trace with a size 2–1/0 hook on the business end and a small hook threaded on the trace as a retainer (see diagram). This arrangement supports the bait during the casting and leaves the large hook clear for clean penetration on the strike.

Rudd, Roach, Bream, Perch and Chub

For pike fishing in shallow waters where bottom weed proves troublesome, I rate small rudd, again around the 5–7in mark, by far the best choice because they keep working vigorously exclusively in the upper water layers. Incidentally, nowadays I never use livebaits longer than 7 in. Since these small fish will work attractively for long periods if presented

Hooking on 5-7 inch freshwater livebaits like rudd, roach, bream, perch and chub.

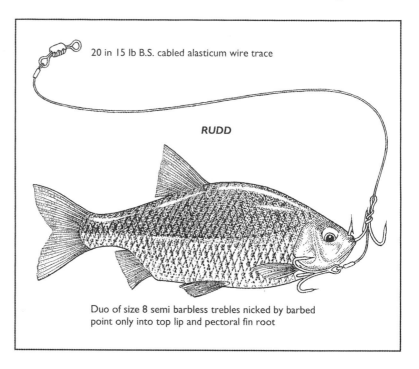

20 in 15 lb B.S. cabled alasticum wire trace

RUDD

Duo of size 8 semi barbless trebles nicked by barbed point only into top lip and pectoral fin root

on sensitive float tackle and a well-greased line, I cannot see the point in using anything larger. Why use quality livebaits — possibly someone else's prize catch — which pike all too often have trouble turning and merely maul before dropping, when, with a smaller bait, an almost instant strike can be made?

My largest-ever pike, weighing over 30 lb, came to a 5 in rudd from Norfolk's River Thurne system, where weed is invariably a problem even during the winter. This disposes of the theory put about by some fishermen that you can catch big pike only on big baits.

Roach are the obvious livebait choice, being the most common shoal fish of all and part of almost every pike's daily diet. Bream are good too, and with that extra depth to their body, send out exaggerated distress signals when working strongly. Bream x roach hybrids are even better because they have more stamina.

Perch are overlooked, especially by the young pike anglers, possibly on account of the complete fallacy that pike won't eat them because of their prickly dorsal fin. What a load of rubbish! I wish I had a fiver for every small perch that has produced a pike for me over the years.

Perch work doggedly too, and last well if not repeatedly cast. However, they have a habit of swimming into the sub-surface snags, so beware. An old saying which is perfectly true is that 'big perch love little perch'. But don't be tempted into presenting them on a wire trace if you are after a big perch, just in case a pike happens along. While adult perch are not fooled by wire and a set of trebles very often, use a size 4 single hook tied direct to 6-lb line and hook the bait once only through the top lip of both nostrils (see diagram).

Chub are, without question, the strongest of this group of livebaits, but are not an easy fish to locate in profusion within most river systems. My local river, the Wensum, for instance, contains wonderful stocks of chub in the 3–4½ lb bracket, but I honestly could not tell you, even if my life depended on it, where to catch a dozen 6-in chub.

Common, Mirror and Crucian Carp

When available — and some ponds do breed these small carp well beyond manageable numbers — carp in the 5–7 in range are very active baits which will work attractively for hours.

Trout

As a winter sideline, many fish farmers offer live rainbow trout of various sizes from 3 to 8in to pike and zander fishermen at a sensible price. Compared with purchasing maggots, not forgetting the cost of your petrol there and back simply to catch a few dace or roach, farmed trout make sense costwise.

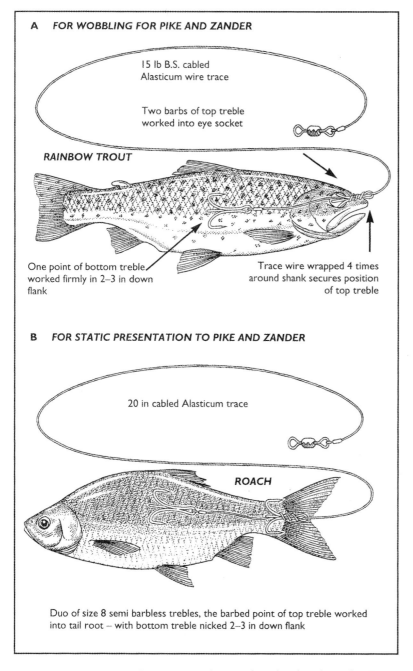

A *FOR WOBBLING FOR PIKE AND ZANDER*

15 lb B.S. cabled
Alasticum wire trace

Two barbs of top treble
worked into eye socket

RAINBOW TROUT

One point of bottom treble
worked firmly in 2–3 in down
flank

Trace wire wrapped 4 times
around shank secures position
of top treble

B *FOR STATIC PRESENTATION TO PIKE AND ZANDER*

20 in cabled Alasticum trace

ROACH

Duo of size 8 semi barbless trebles, the barbed point of top treble worked
into tail root – with bottom treble nicked 2–3 in down flank

**Hooking on
freshwater deadbaits
like dace, rudd, roach,
chub and rainbow
trout.**

But you must, of course, first check the local Water
Authority's ruling on the transportation and use of trout as
livebait in an alien water.

Freshwater Deadbaits

All of the previously mentioned livebaits work well as static
deadbaits if wrapped individually and quickly frozen until
required. As do grayling, a species I have yet to use as a

115

This comprehensive selection of frozen deadbaits, both natural and coloured, includes sprats, smelts, joey and large mackerel, herrings, sandeels, trout and horse mackerel.

livebait, because only during the winter months when long-trotting southern chalk streams do I come across the species in quantity. In fact, in most cases only in return for taking them away do I ever gain access to some of the choicest beats on the wonderful winding streams of Berkshire and Hampshire.

Friendly river keepers would always much rather thin out the grayling of trout fisheries by using rod and line, as opposed to electrofishing, which tends to destroy and disturb the aquatic insect life on which trout feed.

For wobbling, however, and the repeated casting it involves, only the more solid species, such as dace, rudd, roach, chub and rainbow trout, are advisable. Mount any of these on a duo of size 8 treble hooks with two barbs of the top treble worked into the eye socket, and one barb of the bottom treble embedded firmly into the flank 2–3-in away (see diagram). For presenting the static deadbait, reverse the procedure, working one barb of the top treble into the bait's

When presented completely static on the bottom, very large deadbaits can be cut diagonally and used as half baits, so that their juices permeate through the water faster. Small baits, however, are best used whole, particularly when being wobbled.

Eels usually prefer a freshwater natural bait, although occasionally they will accept a small seabait. This three-and-a-half-pounder, for instance, gobbled up a sprat intended for catfish.

117

**Right and opposite:
Hooking on eel
deadbaits.**

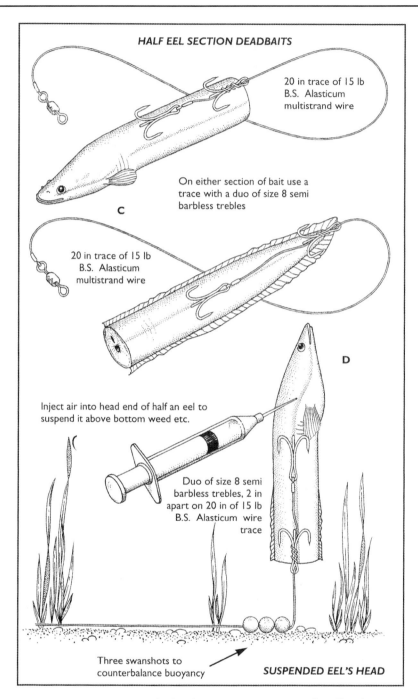

HALF EEL SECTION DEADBAITS

20 in trace of 15 lb
B.S. Alasticum
multistrand wire

On either section of bait use a
trace with a duo of size 8 semi
barbless trebles

C

20 in trace of 15 lb
B.S. Alasticum
multistrand wire

D

Inject air into head end of half an eel to
suspend it above bottom weed etc.

Duo of size 8 semi
barbless trebles, 2 in
apart on 20 in of 15 lb
B.S. Alasticum wire
trace

Three swanshots to
counterbalance buoyancy

SUSPENDED EEL'S HEAD

sinewy tail root, and the bottom one into the flank (see diagram).

Another species I rate very highly indeed for deadbaiting, though I don't think I would have the bottle to present one live, is the eel. In most river systems this is easily caught during the summer and can be frozen for use during the winter. Eel fishermen, who use Dutch fyke nets, will, I'm sure,

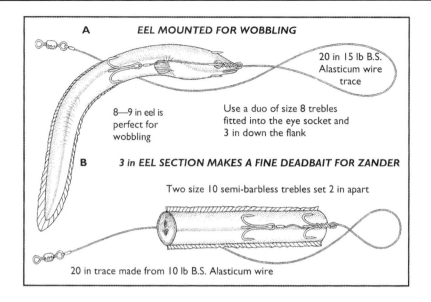

A   EEL MOUNTED FOR WOBBLING

20 in 15 lb B.S.
Alasticum wire
trace

8—9 in eel is
perfect for
wobbling

Use a duo of size 8 trebles
fitted into the eye socket and
3 in down the flank

B   3 in EEL SECTION MAKES A FINE DEADBAIT FOR ZANDER

Two size 10 semi-barbless trebles set 2 in apart

20 in trace made from 10 lb B.S. Alasticum wire

also oblige you with a supply. And should you see a dragline working on river, lake or canal, look among the pile of bottom silt which the shoe deposits on the bank. It will be full of eels.

As for size, eels in the 8-14-in bracket make perfect pike baits. I use the shorter ones whole for wobbling (see diagram) and cut the larger ones in half for use as static deadbaits. Incidentally, a 3-in section of an eel 12-14 in long mounted on a duo of size 10 trebles to 10 lb cabled Alasticum, makes the perfect static deadbait for the finicky zander (see diagram). Some zander specialists actually prefer eel sections to gudgeon.

You can also mount half eels (see diagram). To suspend this super bait so that it hovers tantalizingly just above bottom weed or silt, try injecting a little air into the head with a hypodermic syringe (see diagram).

Not only is this entirely free natural bait mustard for pike, zander and catfish — though I have yet to catch a perch on an eel section — you are not likely to upset anyone by collecting a batch.

There is a marked difference in smell between freshly killed dead fish and those stored (especially for too long) in a freezer. If a human can differentiate between them, the difference to a fish must be really acute. This undoubtedly explains why some fishermen never achieve satisfactory or consistent results with deadbaits.

Unfortunately we are not always able to use freshly killed fish, and must often put our faith in the freezer and in baits stored not in a mass but wrapped individually in clingfilm or polythene bags, so that we need only defrost enough for a day's pike fishing. Freezing a whole batch of freshly killed deadbaits in one lump, all covered in bits of grass, slime and

119

Above: Deadbaits may be coloured easily and effectively with liquid food dyes. Brush on the colour straight from the bottle and allow each fish to dry before freezing.

Right: Presenting the static sea deadbait for pike.

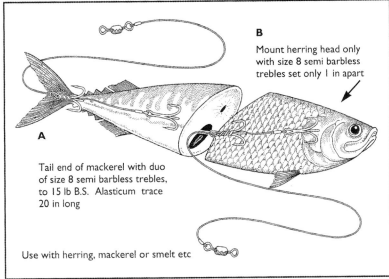

B
Mount herring head only with size 8 semi barbless trebles set only 1 in apart

A
Tail end of mackerel with duo of size 8 semi barbless trebles, to 15 lb B.S. Alasticum trace 20 in long

Use with herring, mackerel or smelt etc

loose scales, and wrapped loosely in newspaper, is an utter waste of time and of a valuable resource.

Sea Deadbaits

The scent of many sea fishes such as the cucumber-smelling smelt, sprats, herrings and mackerel, with their very special and individual aroma, definitely turns pike on. Indeed there are times when sea species easily outfish freshwater naturals.

To colour deadbaits with powder carp bait dyes, swish them around in a two-pint bait tin, holding the tail firmly with forceps.

Using a large-bore hypodermic needle, you can inject all manner of attractors into your deadbaits to jazz them up.

Once again, the secret of success and encouraging pike to suck up your deadbait from the bottom, is to offer the freshest fish available. Therefore, before buying fish from your local wet fish shop or the market, look carefully at their gills, which should be bright red and not pale grey. The overall appearance should be bright, not dull.

Put your bait fish in the freezer at once, wrapped individually in clingfilm or in polythene bags. But if you haven't space in your freezer, most specialist tackle shops these days stock an entire range of blast-frozen, well-packaged

121

sea deadbaits such as sardines, horse mackerel, mullet and sandeels, as well as the favourites already mentioned.

Oddball sea species, such as the colourful gurnard, red mullet and Mediterranean sea bream — and in fact, virtually any fresh fish — are worth trying. All will catch when presented static or drifted off the bottom beneath a float. But for wobbling, those with really firm flesh are better, such as small (joey) mackerel, mullet or horse mackerel.

In recent years pike fishermen have enjoyed good results with squid and even baby octopus. They may look strange, but pike wolf them down just as they would any other tasty morsel of flesh lying on the bottom providing an easy meal. Baby squid, incidentally, are a fabulous wobbling bait. Give them a try.

Presenting sea fish as deadbaits is no different from using freshwater species. It is simply a matter of relating size of the trebles to that of the bait (see diagram). To mount a sprat, use a duo of size 10 hooks and a half mackerel — or 'mackerel tail' as it is better known, by far the most dense and longest casting deadbait — a duo of size 8s, or 6s with a large mackerel.

A point worth mentioning here is that while everyone tends to present just the tail end if fishing 'half baits', there is absolutely no reason whatsoever for ignoring the heads (see diagram). I have enjoyed tremendous success with herring heads in the coloured waters of my local Norfolk Broads, including one memorable November day which saw three pike over the magical 20-lb mark hoisted into the boat. Each succumbed to just the head of a herring presented static on the bottom beneath a sliding-float rig and a pair of size 8 semi-barbless trebles.

Colouring Deadbaits

Colouring your pike baits, be they from the sea or freshwater, with either neat liquid food colouring or the powder dyes used for making carp baits, offers an interesting challenge to those who regularly fish in clear waters, or where the pike wise up as a result of over-fishing. And let's make no bones about it: pike may well have teeth-studded jaws, but they can be just as choosy about what they eat - its freshness, its colour and the way it is presented - as carp.

My favourite colours for dyeing pike baits are red and yellow, which both show up really well. Yellow, or a bright, intense gold, is especially useful when wobbling or presenting statics in water with a heavy greenish tint. But no doubt you will have your own preferences.

Colouring could not be easier. Place the batch of freshly bought (or caught) baits to be coloured on newspaper on the kitchen table or work surface and thoroughly blot off all

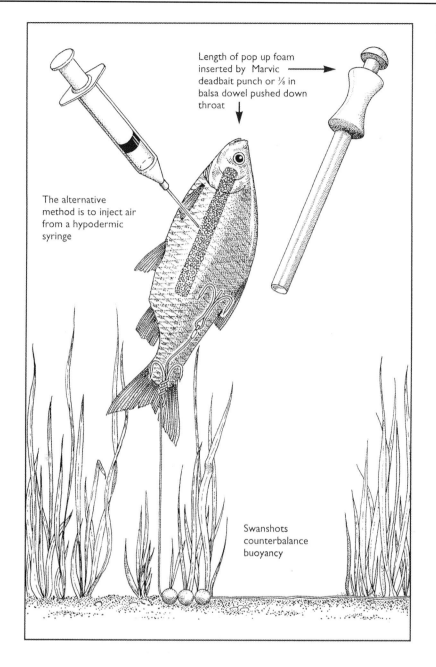

Suspending deadbaits above bottom weeds.

Length of pop up foam inserted by Marvic deadbait punch or ⅛ in balsa dowel pushed down throat

The alternative method is to inject air from a hypodermic syringe

Swanshots counterbalance buoyancy

excess water with kitchen roll. Apply neat food colouring with a brush on both sides of each fish and allow this to dry before wrapping the fish in clingfilm or polythene bags and popping them in the freezer.

The powder dye should be mixed with water in a two-pint bait box (a level teaspoon to half a pint of water) and the fish, gripped by the tail with artery forceps, is swished slowly back and forth on both sides until the overall colour is even.

123

Injecting Deadbaits

Immediately before casting, there are two more tricks available, assuming you have correctly frozen and possibly coloured your deadbaits. One is to suspend the bait off the bottom either by inserting balsa dowel, or pop-up foam (the Marvic deadbait punch makes an easier job of this) or by injecting air into it with a hypodermic syringe. The second is to inject the bait with an attractor oil.

I have always been of the opinion that it is the individual scent of the deadbait which is the attractor, provided it is fished as fresh as possible. Nevertheless, many large pike do succumb to deadbaits that have been injected with concentrated fish-oil attractors derived from prime scad, freshwater eel, squid, kipper, smelt, grey mullet, sardine, pilchard, herring, and so on. Any of these oils may be easily injected directly into the centre of the bait. Apply a good squirt with a large-bore hypodermic syringe. If you feel more confident spicing up your deadbaits with attractors, this fact alone should ensure greater success.

CHAPTER SEVEN

ARTIFICIAL LURES

Last, but by no means least, we come to the countless permutations of wood, aluminium, copper, brass, stainless steel, perspex, plastic, rubber, wool, fur and feather which collectively come under the heading of artificial lures. There are literally thousands of individual patterns, with more available all the time, and it would take a book in itself to discuss every one.

Instead I shall do the next best thing and try to categorize lures according to the purpose for which they were designed,

The variation in size, colour and action of spinners, spinning jigs and plastic worms, is quite staggering, as this selection demonstrates. Simply collecting them can be fun.

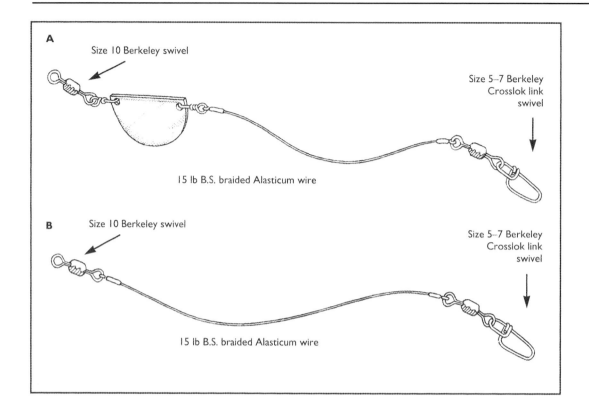

A

Size 10 Berkeley swivel

Size 5–7 Berkeley
Crosslok link
swivel

15 lb B.S. braided Alasticum wire

B

Size 10 Berkeley swivel

Size 5–7 Berkeley
Crosslok link
swivel

15 lb B.S. braided Alasticum wire

Spinning traces.

as well as describing a few favourites. My reason for doing this is that trying to work out the function for which a lure has been created — for instance, the depth to which a plug of a particular shape will dive — is the eternal problem faced by the customer gazing in amazement at the vast display of artificial lures in the local tackle shop.

Spinners

As producers of small spinners, the French firms of Rublex and Mepps have had the entire market virtually sewn up for many years, and it must be said that their choice in spinners of all shapes and weights is mind-boggling. Most spinners are based on the flashing, tantalizing, vibrating action produced by a blade or spoon which revolves, often at high speed, around a weighted bar system. Incidentally, kinks in the line can prove a serious problem when using a spinner, and the best way to eradicate this is to incorporate a plastic anti-kink vane when constructing your spinning traces from braided Alasticum wire.

For pike or zander fishing, I use 15 lb wire with a size 10 Berkeley swivel on the anti-kink vane (which is tied to the reel line) and a size 5–7 Berkeley Croslok snap swivel tied at the lure end, allowing a rapid switch from one lure to another (see diagram). When expecting perch or chub, you have the option

126

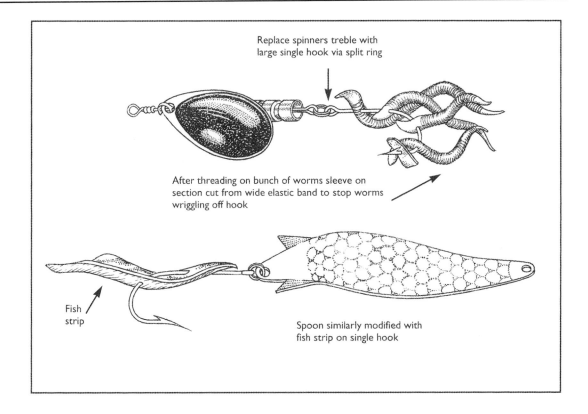

Replace spinners treble with
large single hook via split ring

After threading on bunch of worms sleeve on
section cut from wide elastic band to stop worms
wriggling off hook

Fish
strip

Spoon similarly modified with
fish strip on single hook

Baiting spinners.

of reducing wire strength or using a plain monofilament trace
from the reel line, which nearly always induces more hits.

With certain patterns of spinners, such as Voblex, whose
rubbery head acts as a built-in anti-kink vane, and Eppinger's
Dardevle spinner, the stem of which is bent up almost at right
angles, anti-kink vanes are, of course, unnecessary.

Small Mepps spinners such as the Aglia fly and Comet range,
plus ABU's Droppen and Reflex and similar patterns such as
the famous Veltic and Ondex made by Rublex, and Landa
Flipz-X, which have brilliantly coloured fluorescent blades, in
sizes 0 to 2, are all fabulous perch, zander and chub catchers.

Even the occasional large pike finds the high-speed whirring
action of these tiny spinners irresistible. If you have pike only
in mind, sizes from 3 upwards are ideal. Also excellent for
pike, with enough weight for long casting, are Mepps Lusox
which has a thick woollen red tail and a lead head (which acts
as a built-in anti-kink vane) and Mepps Aglia Longue in sizes 3,
4 and 5.

I have used these particular spinners with great results on
Zimbabwe's famous Zambezi River and in Lake Kariba for the
legendary tiger fish. To improve hooking — treble hooks get
caught up in the tiger fish's array of teeth — the treble was
replaced by a large single hook, heavily baited with redworms. This technique makes predators hang on that much

127

longer, and I suggest you try it for chub and perch. To stop worms wriggling off the large single hook, slip on a short section cut from a wide elastic band (see diagram).

With pike specifically in mind, exchange the worms for a length of fresh fish strip. Again, because of the smell and texture of the flesh, pike will hold on to the spinner that much longer before letting go. And you will be surprised at the effectiveness of a large single replacing the treble hook.

I have been fortunate enough to fish in Canada in recent years, working spinners and spoons in huge, deep lakes for giant lake trout and pike, where the rules permit only a single, barbless hook. Initially I was concerned about fish coming off, but, if anything, I probably landed more fish on the single, barbless hook than if I had used trebles. The two keys to success are not allowing the line to go slack and keeping the hook point honed to a fine edge — one reason why a small file has a permanent place in my fishing waistcoat.

I'm afraid I have digressed a little, but for good reason. So back to spinners. During the 1980s an important innovation improved the simple-bladed bar spinner: someone had the brilliant idea of extending the stem and covering it in a length of latex tubing. Hey presto, the 'flying condom' was born.

Salmon fishermen quickly took to this hybrid, along with

Above: For the widest choice in spinner baits and the outlandish surface-churning buzzbaits, seek out specialist tackle shops which stock American-style artificial lures.

Opposite: John took this 14 lb tiger fish from Zimbabwe's famous Zambezi River during the filming of his *Go Fishing* series. He used a large spinner baited with fish strip — a technique that works equally well with our perch and pike.

129

the highly effective technique of casting upstream and retrieving the 'condom' back downstream and across the flow. On Irish rivers, where the device is widely used, I have enjoyed superb sport on the Rivers Bann, Moy and Shannon, where, in addition to salmon, a fair number of pike have also happened along.

That the condom is now here to stay as a classic lure, I have absolutely no doubt — in its original form with a latex tube of either red or natural, plus versions which sport soft plastic fish, or bodies of traditional bucktail flies. In addition to pike, zander, big perch and chub all hit condoms with equal confidence.

A complete contrast to small-bladed spinners, the now rather outdated Colorado and kidney spinners, firm favourites with pike fishers of yesteryear, still catch as well as ever, but have inevitably suffered at the hands of fashion. However, for those odd occasions when all else fails and you are faced with an excessive distance to cast or deep, fast water to explore, a Colorado or kidney spoon (which actually revolves) among your lures could prove invaluable.

I have deliberately not gone into blade colour — whether gold, silver or bronze, spotted, striped or flecked, and so on, is best. The permutations are too complex for me to be dogmatic about choice. Confidence in your own ability is the most important factor, plus using a lure of the correct type and weight to combat the prevailing conditions.

Spinner Baits

These unique contraptions evolved by American black-bass fishermen and consisting of a V-shaped frame to which a vibrating spoon, rubber skirt and large single-eyed hook are fixed, work just as effectively in British waters for perch, zander, chub and pike.

Since nothing on a spinner bait actually spins, an anti-kink vane is not necessary, and a simple-wire trace with a snap swivel at the business end (see diagram) is all you need to work them, and every lure mentioned from now on.

On a number of my spinner baits, I have wired to the single-eyed hook a size 6 treble, which increases the hooking rate when pike are coming short. This does cancel out the weed-free action of this particular lure, but then you can't have everything. I particularly like the wide range of spinner baits made by the Blue Fox Tackle Co, Barries Buzzer and Double Buzzer made by Ryobi Masterline, and the Tandem Spin by Mepps. For the very best choice of spinner baits, find a specialist tackle shop with a comprehensive stock of American lures.

Spinner baits excel in heavily coloured waters, especially in deep lakes, because they can be retrieved really slowly but still emit strong, vibratory pulses. Those with double blades create enormous vibrations, and the spinner-bait kits, which include a selection of different coloured blades and rubber skirts, are a sound investment. As with many of today's lures, spinner baits are also available with plastic fish or frogs instead of the rubber skirt, and the smaller sizes, apart from being great fun, are really useful for perch and chub.

Spinning Jigs and Soft Worms

These have a similar but much shorter frame than spinner baits, incorporating a vibratory blade plus a lead-headed jig on to which either plastic worms or fish may be sleeved. For chub and perch, these little artificials are electric and great fun with a super-light outfit.

I love to use soft plastic worms rigged with a large single hook for chub. If the point is only just nicked into the soft plastic, with the shank threaded through the worm's head, they are completely weedless, and may be twitched and jerked through the thickest surface weed. For working close to the bottom in deep runs, pinch a swan shot tight up against the worm's head so that it flutters straight down each time you pause during the retrieve.

Buzzbaits

If popping artificials along the surface for chub and pike turns you on as it does me, then don't set off without at least one or two buzzbaits among your collection. Built so that the propeller churns the surface film to make predators look up, many buzzbaits come fitted with fine-wire weed guards so that they can be worked through virtually any underwater jungle. I rate the Buzz 'n' Devle, Uncle Buck's Buzzer, Brush Popper, Clacker and Sputterbuzz as among the best.

Spoons

In large, shallow stillwaters where weed grows thick to just below the surface, I love to use weedless spoons and flutter them in with a fast, erratic retrieve. those incorporating a large, feather-covered single hook protected by a sprung wireguard, such as Eppinger's Dardevle Weedless or the Toby Vass, or Kuusamo's Professor Weedless, are highly recommended.

Having accumulated various sizes and colours from pike fishing in North America, I would put Dardevle's 4-in model in either chartreuse or red and white at the top of the list. One of my all-time-favourite spoons, ABU's Atom, a deep-sided, ribbed spoon, is also available weedless in the 20-gm size only. As with spinner baits and buzzbaits, for the best choice of weedless spoons and other surface artificials, seek out tackle shops which specialize in American lures.

131

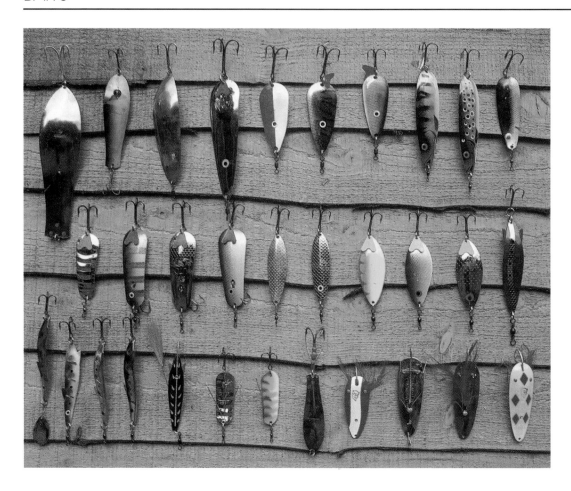

Among this comprehensive selection of spoons are: first row, left to right: Kuusamo Professor, copper Vincent, Kilty Heron and Mikki spoons, Landa Pikko-Fatta Longa; second row: ABU Atom, UTO, Koster, Big Wiggley, Toby; third row: Landa Lukki and Flipz, ABU weedless Toby Vass and Atoms, Kuusamo Professor Weedless, weedless spoons from Dardevle.

Now for spoons in general, which I think are the most versatile of all artificials. As I have just mentioned, ABU's Atom is an excellent all-round choice available in sizes 12—35 gm. But there is an enormous ABU collection. The Big Wiggley, for instance, a deep-sided model introduced in 1992, has a superb wobbling action and is available in a range of weights and unusual colours from plain silver to fluorescent yellow. Supplied with two trebles, the UTO is also a great pike catcher in the 35-gm size, but the second treble can prove troublesome, so simply take it off if it repeatedly flips back over the trace.

The famous Toby, now copied by everyone, catches pike (and perch in the 7—12-gm sizes) everywhere, and is easily cast long distances. The Koster, however, which is available up to 40 gm, casts like the proverbial bullet, though this action really only permits a fast retrieve unless you are working a deep, fast river.

While on the subject of large spoons, a particular pattern has been successful for me. For trolling on big waters as far apart as Ireland's Lough Corrib and Lake Nueltin in Canada,

132

They may look plain and simple, yet when presented correctly and at the right depth, big spoons catch big pike, as John proves with this meaty gravel pit fish of 20 lb-plus.

and, of course, when pike fishing my local Norfolk Broads, I used the Pikko — Fatta Longa, made by Landa. These spoons have a most attractive trout/perch finish on one side and come in sizes from 20 to 35 gm suitable for working both extreme shallows and deep waters. Incidentally, Landa's Toby lookalikes (the Lukki and Turbo spoons) come in a superb range of spectacular colours. These same lures are also available, as the Lukki and Flipz, sporting a spinning blade up front. They are well worth a try.

The Kilty Lure Co of Ireland also produces some extremely useful large spoons. For all-round sport, and weighing a substantial 32 gm, the Miki spoon is a great caster. But for those who require a really big spoon for particular situations, and I do mean big, try the Heron, which is available in four sizes from 30 to 100 gm and in six colours. Another superb, really large spoon (60 gm) with a lovely wobbling action especially good for trolling, is the $7\frac{1}{2}$-in long Professor 00 made by Kuusamo. The 27-gm Professor 1H, $4\frac{1}{2}$-in long, is one of the best-actioned spoons on the market. It can even be attached at either end to vary the action.

Among my own collection are numerous oddball spoons of all shapes and sizes (some made from miscellaneous, large spoons purchased at car boot sales) in hammered copper, silver and stainless steel. Copper, especially, tarnishes very quickly indeed, and if there is one lesson to be learnt from spoon fishing, it is to keep them burnished bright for maximum 'flash' and attraction. So keep a cloth and cleaner in your kit. For a quick restoration of tarnished spoons, I have found Peek the most effective cleaner.

Baiting spoons can, on the right day, give you the edge. In clear water, for instance, or when pike are particularly finicky, try replacing the treble with a large single hook to which a 2 or 3-in strip of fish belly or squid is attached.

Surface Plugs and Poppers

Working floating lures through lily pads, along weed lines and over dense weedbeds that cannot be fished by any other method is the most exciting way of catching chub and pike. Such lures do not dive, but gurgle, pop, splutter and chug, displacing the surface film and drawing predators upwards out of their hide-outs to attack. Many seem utterly preposterous, for instance, Heddon's famous Crazy Crawler, which flip-flops in a crippled butterfly stroke — but it turns pike absolutely crazy.

Other Heddon patterns I recommend are the Torpedo (best in red and white) which has a propeller at the rear, and the Dying Flutter, sporting one at each end. Both are best retrieved in short, sharp bursts. The Zara Spook, which produces real slamming hits, should also be retrieved fast, by jerking the rod tip from side to side. The smaller Chugger Spook, with its popping, gurgling action, is a great pike and chub catcher.

So too, is the Zara Mouse, which incorporates a rattle and a large, single hook at the rear, protected by a weed guard. It goes through the thickest of surface weedbeds. The Creek Chub Mouse, which has a long hair tail and a wedge-shaped head that gurgles beautifully, is another firm top-water favourite. Also from Heddon is the unusual Throbber, a transparent surface lure incorporating an internal spring designed to simulate vibrations similar to those produced by wounded fish.

A different, yet most effective, top-water pattern for both chub and pike among weeds is Rebel's Buzz 'n' Frog, the rear legs of which rotate to really churn the surface. Equally oddball is Mann's Ghost, a highly buoyant, soft plastic tube with a large double hook cleverly fitted so that only when chomped will the points catch. This feature makes the ghost completely weed-free regardless of surface greenery. Try it in fluorescent yellow.

I can't possibly end this section — although, of course, there is no way of mentioning everyone's favourite — without suggesting you try Luhr Jensen's Bass Oreno. This heavy, top-water special casts like a dream and will zoom several inches below the surface in a tantalizing side-to-side motion, as well as gurgling and popping on the top.

Floating Divers

This group amounts to the largest, and certainly the most versatile of all plugs,whether single, double or treble-jointed. Some dive between just 1 and 3 ft when retrieved, while others, such as Mann's Bait Company's revolutionary 'depth plus series', incorporate huge plastic lips (or diving vanes) which zoom down to 10 ft and more after just two or three cranks of the reel handle. Over on the other side of the Atlantic, floating divers are better known as 'crank baits'. and in all cases, it is the plug's 'lip' which indicates how deep it will work — the bigger these are, the deeper it dives.

For chub especially, though both also catch pike in plenty, I like Ryobi's Mugger (particularly in silver) and Shakespeare's Big S range, including the Midi S and Small S, all of which have ball-bearing rattles. This particular shape is used by countless manufacturers, including Mann's Bait Company in its Baby 1—minus and 1—minus, which casts like a bullet.

Normark's Shad Rap Shallow Runner is another firm favourite, available in four sizes and five colours. Try it in 'firetiger'. Along the more overgrown parts of my local River Wensum, Heddon's Meadow Mouse always induces a few

135

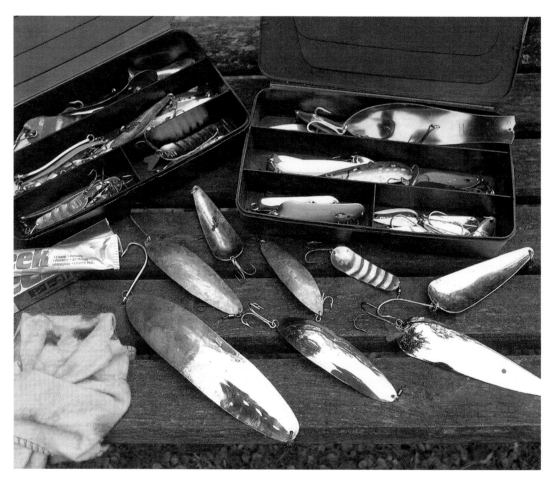

It is the action and their distinct 'flash' which attracts predators to spoons so don't let them become tarnished. Restore their brilliance regularly with a strong paste-type cleaner and a soft cloth.

Opposite: These American popping lures all have one thing in common: they create those irritating, 'wounded fish' pulses which bring pike quickly up to the surface for an attack.

takes from both pike and chub, but the most unlikely plug of all is surely Heddon's Big Budd, which looks like a beer can crossed with a spinner. It always provokes insults from friends, but the smile soon leaves their faces when pike start grabbing hold. It is a super lure that I would not fancy leaving at home.

If you like highly reflective lures, then the L Jack Minnow from Yo-Zuri is another great choice — a shallow diver with a side-to-side wiggle, available in five sizes between 3 and 7 in. For working both clear and coloured water, I love this particular lure in hot orange. A floating diver with a very similar, but accentuated side-to-wide wiggle, is the Riplin Redfin from Cotton Cordell. Its unusual action is attributable to a body which is rippled along both sides.

For exploring greater depths, Normark's Rattl'n Fat Rap, Rapala's Fat Rap Deep Runner and Shad Rap Deep Runner, and Mann's 10+ all have great vibratory actions while diving to 10 ft or more. If you want to go deeper still, Mann's 15+, 20+ and the incredible 30+ are the lures to have. The 20+ Deep Hog is, in fact, the first floating/diving lure ever created that is

guaranteed to reach depths of 20 ft or more. It dives almost vertically on the retrieve. The 30+ will actually go deeper — to over 40 ft when trolled with 75 yards of line out. Both are perfect for exploring the undulating, irregular bottom contours of really deep gravel pits.

A lure that will also reach good depths when trolled at medium speed is Heddon's Magnum Tadpolly. It comes in two sizes, and is a great pattern for coloured water because it sends out massive vibrations, even when retrieved slowly. Similar in action is the banana-shaped Lazy Ike, available in 3 and 3 ½-in models that dive on even a slow retrieve down to 8 or 9 ft. Two superb lures I regularly use are the Shadlings from the Lindy 'Little Joe' Inc. Made from high-density plastic, these 6-in super-strong lures cast exceptionally well. The shallow diver goes down to 7–8 ft, while you can get down to 20 ft with the huge-lipped deep diver.

I also like the hand-crafted, balsa-wood lures made by Nilsmaster of Finland. They cast like bullets and have great lifelike actions. Two I recommend are the 7-in Invincible, which dives to 8 ft, and the 6-in Invincible-DR, which, with its stainless-steel vane, is built for deep diving, but can also be worked as a shallow-diving wiggler with a most tantalizing side-to-side movement.

If you prefer the action of jointed plugs, then go for the Eskimo Wobbler from DAM, which comes in double and treble-jointed models. These unusual plugs cast well and dive to several feet in an unusual, tantalizing and quivering action. In fluorescent red and yellow, they really turn pike on.

The Rapala 'jointed floating' pattern also has a superb lifelike action, and comes in a choice of four sizes and seven colours. Blue mackerel is my favourite.

A large and powerful deep diver I regularly use in pits, reservoirs and especially when trolling in saltwater tropics because it is so effective for jacks and barracuda, is Bagley's Monster Shad. And last, but by no means least, because there is an enormous choice in this particular group of lures, I rate the Water Dog and Classic Minnow from the Hawgboss stable.

Sinking Divers

Once allowed to sink to the desired depth, sinking divers stay deep down throughout the retrieve. What's more, certain models, such as ABU's Killer and Rapala's Countdown, available in both single and jointed formats, can be counted down (at around one second per foot of descent) just like a spoon, to the desired depth. I particularly like the Rapalas, which come in several colours and in lengths from 3 to 5 in.

The Rattl'n Rapala is another great sinking diver which stays deep throughout the retrieve regardless of speed. It comes in a super range of bright, reflective colours, and the silver, gold and blue finishes are very effective. A similar lure, the Ratt'l Spot, is made by Cotton Cordell. But my favourite is Rapala's Sliver, which is actually a jointed saltwater lure made of African odom wood and patterned after the needlefish. Needless to say, its joints and hooks are super-strong, so it will deal with the largest pike. The Sliver comes in two sizes, and the smaller, at $5\frac{1}{2}$ in, is simply perfect. Try it in fluorescent yellow or red and white.

If you regularly fish in deep water and prefer the extra strength of saltwater plugs, I suggest you try Rapala's three smallest Sinking Magnums, which, at $3\frac{1}{2}$, $4\frac{1}{2}$ and $5\frac{1}{2}$ in, must be the toughest pike lures on the market. My favourite is the $4\frac{1}{2}$ in model in blue mackerel. These plugs even withstand munching from the teeth of barracuda, as my heavily scarred collection proves. The Yo-Zuri 'jointed sinking' plugs are also worth trying, being available in three lengths from $3\frac{1}{2}$ to $5\frac{1}{2}$ in, and several colours. There is a strong, saltwater deep runner too, called the L—Jack Magnum, which has an attractive, highly reflective body and comes in five sizes from 3 to 7 in and four colours. Orange and blue are my favourites. Yo-Zuri's compact Vibrastar Sinker, which is decidedly Big S in shape, has a translucent, hollow body full of coloured beads, casts well, sinks like a stone, and because of a ball-bearing in the head chamber, sends out enormous vibrations. Like all the Yo-Zuri plugs, it is fitted with excellent hooks.

A great pair of deep-water divers are the Canadian Wiggler and Jointed Wiggler, available in a staggering selection of colour patterns. They are made from brass, and so sink quickly to the desired depth. For something completely different, try Rebel's Sinking Crayfish. It is a great lure for weirpool chub and perch, which pike just can't leave alone. Another great American lure is the Zara Gossa from Heddon, which is a double-jointed sinker, designed not to dive but dance and wiggle through the upper water layers. The Arc Minnow from Yo-Zuri is another good slow sinker for shallow-water work.

Abu Garcia's Jointed Hi-Lo is a very versatile sinker. Fitted with an adjustable six-position diving vane, it can be chugged and wiggled through the surface film over weeds, or wobbled slowly along at any depth you choose.

Finally, it is impossible to write anything on the subject of artificial lures without mentioning that classic American pike catcher, the Creek Chub Pikie. It is available in both single and double-jointed formats and several colours, the red and white being my favourite. This slow-sinking plug is extremely versatile. You can wobble it in quite fast just a couple of feet below the surface, or allow it to sink to the desired depth, before slowly retrieving it. The tantalizing, irritating side-to-side motion leaves pike no choice but to attack.

139

Floating divers are the most versatile of all artificial lures. This is a selection of John's favourites.
First row, left to right: Mann's 30+, Classic Minnow, Ryobi Mugger, Shadling Deep Diver; second row: Mann's 20+ Deep Hog, Waterdog, Big S, Shadling Medium Diver; third row: Mann's 10+, Eskimo Jointed, Shad Rap Shallow Runner, Monster Shad; fourth row: Mann's 5+, Eskimo Wobbler, L Jack Minnow, Shad Rap Deep Runner; fifth row: Mann's 1– minus, Riplin Redfin, L Jack Minnow, Magnum Tadpolly; sixth row: Mann's Baby 1–minus, Big Bud, Invincible DR, Magnum Tadpolly; seventh row: Invincible, Meadow Mouse, Lazy Ike.

A selection of John's sinking divers: first row, top to bottom: Ratt'l
Spot, Rattl'n Rapala, Vibrastar Sinker, Wiggler, Jointed Wiggler;
second row, top to bottom: ABU Hi-lo, Yo-Zuri, L Jack Magnum,
Rapala Sliver, Yo-Zuri Jointed Sinker, Yo-Zuri Ark Minnow; third row,
top to bottom: L Jack Magnum, Sinking Crawfish, ABU Killer,
Countdown, Creek Chub Pikie, Zara Gossa, Rapala Sinking Magnum.

CHAPTER EIGHT

THE 'JERK BAIT' SYNDROME

They say that anything which happens in the USA will inevitably arrive in the UK five or ten years later – depending upon who gives you the quotation – and I guess they, whoever they are, are not far from the truth. It's happened with the electronic mass media age in terms of satellite television and games, CD-ROMs, DVDs and computers. Now it's happened with braided lines and artificial lures, namely the 'jerk bait' syndrome.

Braided lines

Let's start with braided lines, which have revolutionized both line fishing and distance fishing in fresh water throughout the UK. Due to their non-stretch properties and greatly reduced diameter compared to monofilament line of equivalent breaking strain, braided lines have made deep-water sea fishing much more pleasurable. When working deep-water offshore wrecks, for instance, whether drift fishing using artificials or simply fishing at anchor, low-diameter braided lines have opened up a whole new field of more exciting sports fishing.

Whilst braided lines can be used with fixed-spool reels for working spoons and plugs, these fine low-diameter synthetic lines are more effectively used with multiplying reels. And as a general guide, it's wise to use a breaking strain in braid of at least twice what you would use in monofilament, both as a safety precaution (due to the lines being no-stretch) and because braided lines are so low in diameter. For instance, a braided line of say 30lb test is actually thinner than monofilament of 12lb test. So why go lighter? Remember that the slightest nick in an already fine line will greatly reduce its breaking strain. Incidentally, 'fused' and slightly stiffer braided

143

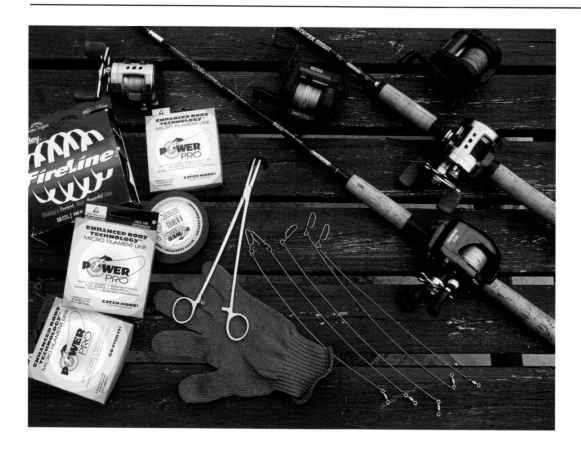

Except for the jerk baits themselves, here is everything you need to enjoy this specialized branch of lure fishing. Hi-tech, fused, braided, low-diameter, non-stretch reel lines, plus long-nosed forceps and Normark unhooking glove. 12 in, single-strand, stainless-steel anti-tangle traces. A selection of Masterline multiplier reels and the stiff one-piece rods required to 'work' jerk baits.

lines are better for working lures than 'soft' braids. For working large and heavy artificials like jerk baits, which start at around 6 in long and go up to 10 in in length, a braided reel line of 50lb test is ideal, and is thinner than 18lb monofilament.

Reels and rods

Multiplier reels best suited for braided lines are those in the 5000–6500 size range. For braid of 30lb test then both Masterline's Toothy Critter and my own John Wilson Super Shooter reels fit the bill admirably. Alternatively, ABU's Ultracast 5601 and Classic 5501 are also proven workhorses. For heavier braids up to 50lb, the Masterline T2 or Shimano Calcutta reels, either the 251 or 400, have a larger capacity. ABU's Ultracast 6501 is another option. Either way the reel should have a robust frame, a smooth sensitive clutch and automatic level line lay.

Rods for working jerk bait lures are in an entirely separate class from all others. They need to be short and stiff, and possess a trigger grip reel seat enabling your forefinger to lock beneath the multiplier while the thumb controls the spool on top of the rod. If you're right-handed, then work the rod with

144

your right hand and wind in with your left. A left-hand wind reel is thus imperative. My own Masterline John Wilson 6 ft Super Shooter jerk-bait rod is ideal for anyone throwing big lures like jerk baits in the 1½–3½ oz range. Going up a step, the Masterline Toothy Critter jerk bait rod available in both 6 and 7 ft models will cast lures up to 4 oz. Two more excellent options are Shimano's 6½ ft Compre and ABU's 6 ft Equalizer Jerk bait.

You see, the main difference between general artificial lures and 'jerk baits' is that most of the former have built-in action through various diving vanes, propellers and contoured body shapes, etc., so that the lure works even when you reel in evenly and slowly. With jerk baits completely the reverse happens, in that most of these larger lures, whether floaters or sinkers, only come alive when worked with short, sharp jerks on the rod tip (hence their name) or with long side-to-side sweeps. A large figure-of-eight movement with the rod tip when the lure is on a short line, close beside the boat for instance, is a proven routine used by North American musky anglers for inducing a dramatic last-ditch take. This is why a really stiff rod and non-stretch braided reel line are essential for transferring every bit of action created by the rod tip on to the artificial. Long, sloppy rods and monofilament lines only absorb and thus suppress rod-tip action, so are useless for working jerk baits. So don't be tempted into purchasing

A comprehensive selection of large jerk baits within the 6–10 in size range, both floaters and sinkers. Note how some models are equipped with rubber tails for extra attraction. All are fitted with large, extra-strong trebles to split rings, for immediate changing of bent or blunt hooks. John's favourite jerk bait rods are shown here. His own Masterline 6 ft Super Shooter and the 7 ft Toothy Critter jerk bait rod, also from the Masterline stable.

145

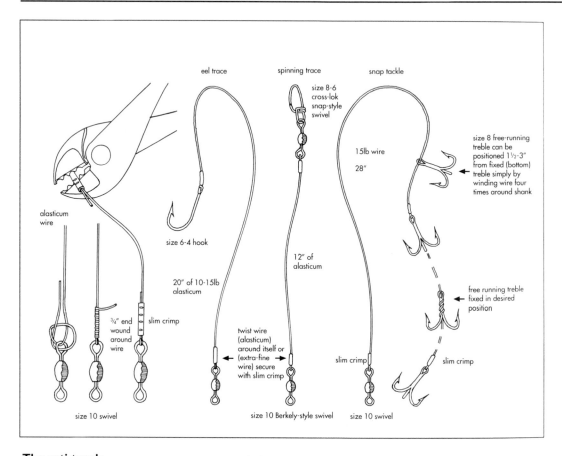

eel trace

spinning trace

snap tackle

size 8-6 cross-lok snap-style swivel

15lb wire

28"

size 8 free-running treble can be positioned 1½-3" from fixed (bottom) treble simply by winding wire four times around shank

alasticum wire

size 6-4 hook

12" of alasticum

free running treble fixed in desired position

20" of 10-15lb alasticum

¾" end wound around wire

slim crimp

twist wire (alasticum) around itself or (extra-fine wire) secure with slim crimp

slim crimp

slim crimp

size 10 swivel

size 10 Berkely-style swivel

size 10 swivel

The anti-tangle, super-strong, 12 in single-strand stainless-steel traces recommended for jerk bait fishing are shown on page 145 and are not home-made. The diagram above, however, provides the DIY fan with customised-trace ideas for converting both alasticum and soft multi-strand wire into swivelled, hook and double-hook traces for the techniques discussed in chapters 6 and 7.

expensive jerk baits and use them on normal spinning gear.

To continue the energy of movement all the way through from rod to lure at the business end, instead of a soft multi-strand wire trace, jerk baits are best presented on a 10–12 in stainless-steel single-strand anti-tangle trace. Remember, this really is an entirely different ball game from general lure fishing. Jerk baits were created in North America for northern pike (our pike) and especially for muskellunge, so everything is specifically geared big for catching big toothy predators. There is an ever growing choice in jerk baits, including floaters, slow sinkers, suspenders and deep divers, as more and more models are imported from North America by specialist tackle suppliers to suit the growing demand of this technique from lure fishing enthusiasts.

It is of course impossible to cover every model, but the following is a rundown on some of my favourites, all of which are proven pike-getters. Incidentally, it is worth mentioning that many jerk baits need to be tuned right out of the package. So start by testing the lure on a straight pull and if it runs off to one side bend the front eye slightly the opposite way. The lure should then run straight and only swing to either side commensurate with rod-tip action.

Jerk-bait lures

Floaters

During the summer months when pike are most likely to attack just below or actually on the surface, buoyant, floating jerk baits are the perfect lure. To see calm water erupt in a shower of spray as a gill-flaring pike catapults itself into a tail-walking sequence completely clear of the surface is what surface fishing is all about. And remember, in the low light values of dawn or dusk pike are even more likely to be on the lookout for an easy meal on the surface beside key habitats, such as reed lines, sunken trees, lily beds, boathouses, beneath bridges etc., etc.

Cobbs floating jerk baits come in a variety of colour patterns from fire tiger to jet black and from 6 to 8 in long. These rounded wooden plugs have a super-smooth finish and, being heavy, cast like a bullet. Cobbs Swimming Minnow, also available in 6 and 8 in versions, is more like a giant large-vaned floating diving plug with an inbuilt side-to-side throbbing action.

The 8 in Burt floating jerk baits from Musky Mania Tackle also come in a range of fancy colour patterns and have a tantalizing side-to-side action. Made from high-impact plastic, these lures are exceptionally durable. The Squirrley Burt has the addition of a lifelike rubber tail. Both lures have built-in rattles and produce best when worked in short pulls. This creates a down-and to-the-side action with a quivering 'hang'.

From the Fish Eagle stable comes the smiling dog floating jerk bait (Reef Hawg) also available in 6 and 8 in models. Available in a variety of colour finishes from orange fire tiger to rainbow trout, these dense wooden lures cast well and come equipped with super sharp trebles.

The Original Pig from Odyssey Lures, a similar shaped floating jerk bait, is another dense wooden lure available in both 6 and 7 in models with built-in rattle and a colour range which includes hot frog, chartreuse bandit and natural perch. Like most floating jerk baits the Pig will zoom beneath the surface to a couple of rapid cranks of the reel handle and swing from side to side in a downwards motion. It then backs up in its own track if given slack on the retrieve.

Sinkers

Sinking jerk baits really come into their own during the winter months for exploring deep-water drop offs where pike could be holding in depths down to 30, 40 and even 50 ft or more. The technique is to use the method of allowing around 1 ft per second whilst mentally counting the lure down to the desired depth before commencing the retrieve. It's such an effectively

147

accurate way of connecting with pike in deep gravel pits and reservoirs. And remember, a slow retrieve in cold water is usually more productive.

The 6 and 8 in Cobb jerk baits are also available in both slow- and fast-sinking models. The fast sinkers are best counted down to the desired depth before starting the retrieve.

The Suspender Pig from Odyssey Lures comes in both 6 and 7 in models plus $4\frac{3}{4}$-in piglet versions. This heavy, easy to cast unusual lure is really a slow sinker which works best down to around 15 ft. After counting it down to the desired depth short 3–6 in twitches on the rod tip will initiate a 'swing'. A 3–5 second pause between jerks will then cause the Pig to hang and stop dead in its tracks – thus its 'suspender' tag. An extremely versatile and most valuable lure to have in your armoury, the Suspender Pig, which comes in a range of colours from natural perch to orange bandit.

An excellent smallish slow sinker that goes down head first is the $6\frac{1}{2}$-in Smity small jerk bait. This wooden lure casts well and is extremely versatile, like all those in the Smith stable. Colour choice available includes chartreuse perch, fire tiger and red horse.

Floating jerk baits – from left to right, top to bottom: Cobbs 6 in floating, Cobbs 8 in floating, Burt 9 in floating, Burt Squirrley Tail floating, Smiling Dog 6 in Reef Hawg floating, Smiling Dog 8 in Reef Hawg floating, Original Pig 7 in Smiling Face floating, Cobbs 8 in Swimming Minnow floating/diver.

Opposite: John prepares to explore the 30 ft deep waters of Grafham's 1,600 acre reservoir for big pike, using an equally big jerk bait. The fabulous 9 in Bull Dawg from Musky Innovations.

One of today's all-time favourite sinking jerk baits is the entirely rubber Bull Dawg from Musky Innovations. Available in both 6 and 9 in models, these flexible lures with built-in twister tail have a hanging treble at the throat, one built into the tail root and a large single protruding from the dorsal, thus providing excellent hook ups. Available in several two-tone colour patterns, the Bull Dawg dives head first quickly and has a great action. Casts well too.

Another simply fascinating deep diver is the 9 in Invader, also from Musky Innovations, which has a plastic head and combined diving vane to which is added a flexible body of dense rubber complete with tail. The Invader sinks head first fast and possesses a throbbing, pluglike action. The two large trebles hang beneath mid-body (one connected to the head and one to the tail) and are joined together with a strong wire link in case the body section is pulled off. This unique lure comes in a variety of colour patterns. A shallow Running Raider with the same specification is also available. This dives to around 6 ft and is in fact an excellent trolling lure.

Perhaps the most unusual of all the fast-sinking jerk baits is the all-rubber Ugly Joe from Live Action Lures. Available in bright yellow, red or black, this totally outrageous and exceptionally heavy lure sinks head first extra fast and has a great wiggly tail action. It can thus be counted down into the deepest swims – 30, 40 ft plus is no problem. The hooking arrangement consists of one large treble hanging from the throat (one prong of which fits into a recess in the belly), a second treble in the tail and a large single protruding from the dorsal. Ugly Joe comes in both small and large sizes.

Lastly, an unusual slow sinker, manufactured in dense see-through plastic, is the pluglike diver from Zalt Lures, which has a built-in rattle and a most erratic action. It casts well and can be retrieved extremely slowly.

Most of these jerk bait lures not only catch pike and muskellunge but other toothy predators around the world. I have enjoyed tremendous success with some of these patterns in Africa whilst catching tigerfish from the Zambezi River, and with vundu catfish and Nile perch in the River Nile itself and within the fast swirling waters at awesome Nurdinson Falls in Uganda. There are also many situations on massive Lake Nasser in Egypt when seeking Nile perch that large jerk baits can really produce the goods. Shore fishing is particularly suited to this style of approach, where, by carefully creeping up along the rocky overhangs, numbers of huge Nile perch can often be seen through Polaroid glasses mere feet below hugging the shade of marginal boulders.

Lures such as the Invader or shallow invader and the all-rubber Bull Dawg then really do irritate these jumbo-sized perch into grabbing hold. Another good Nile perch lure is the

Swimming Minnow from the Cobbs stable.

The only change I make is to replace the bronze trebles of all the lures mentioned with extra-strong plated trebles in 4X wire. 100lb plus Nile perch have unbelievable crunching power.

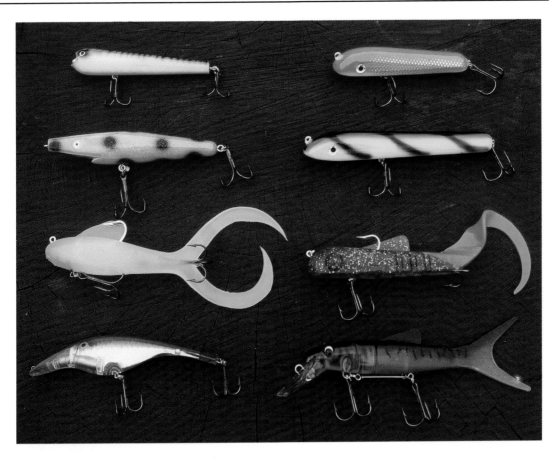

Opposite: Proof of the pudding and small wonder that Wilson's smiling. A huge double-jointed sinking jerk bait in outlandish bright pink accounted for this 18 lb thick-set gravel-pit pike, which grabbed hold close to the bottom in 14 ft of water.

Sinking jerk baits – from left to right, top to bottom: Smity 6 in sinking small jerk, Cobbs 6 in slow sinker, Original Pig 7 in suspender, Cobbs 8 in fast sinker, Large Ugly Joe extra fast sinker, Large Bull Dawg 9 in fast sinker, Zalt jerk plug, Invader 9 in slow sinker.

INDEX

155

The success of jerk bait fishing is not restricted to the predators of temperate waters alone, as John illustrates by playing a big Nile perch hooked amongst the deep and swirling tropical waters of the River Nile at awesome Murchison falls in Uganda.

Overleaf: Yet another
huge Nile perch that
succumbed to a jerk
bait. This near 100-
pounder, helped to
display for the camera
by John's guide,
Joseph, was caught
from Eygpt's massive
Lake Nasser on a
sinking jerk bait whilst
drifting through a
deep-water channel
between weed-clad
islands.